D1015173

Five Star Rating by Readers' Favorite!

Readers' Favorite Review

Difficult Conversations Just for Women: Kill the Anxiety. Get What You Want carries a message that every woman needs to know, especially in this day and age; an expert guide on handling difficult conversations. The title of this book may lure readers into checking it out, but they won't be disappointed. What is most interesting about this book is that it offers just what readers need to know. No fluff, no babbling. It's straightforward talk that will help any woman find their voice and the right approach when dealing with delicate matters, impatient and difficult people, and when they know they have to stand up for themselves but are cowed by the need to please others or fear of rejection.

Sofia Santiago, MBA, PMP and Dr. Susan Harrison are two experts and authorities in the art of communicating effectively, and they bring to this ground-breaking work their many years of research and a rich professional experience. The tone is lively and highly entertaining, and many times readers will find themselves inside the concrete examples and scenarios used to corroborate the salient points of the book. This is one of those rare books that successfully guides readers in the science of communicating in trying moments. It is an excellent tool to help anyone understand the factors that affect effective communication, especially when women have to face men in both business and life, and how to handle emotions in difficult conversations. The message couldn't be timelier!

Difficult Conversations Just for Women: Kill the Anxiety. Get What You Want is a book for every woman, but it is also a book that men need to read. The book is intelligently written, upbeat, and filled with insights that will come across as an eye-opener to many readers. I wish I'd read this book ten years ago, but it is never too late.

— **Readers Favorite**

What WikiWomen™ Are Saying

"*Difficult Conversations Just for Women* had me laughing and learning from start to finish! From the authors' humorous tone to their logical step-by-step processes for helping me get more of what I want in life, I found I couldn't put the book down. Sofia and Susan write in a way that drew me in and made me feel that I've got this 'I am woman; hear me roar!' thing down pat! Thanks for the confidence boost!"

- Tracy

"If you want to understand how men and women deal with things in their lives differently then I suggest you read *Difficult Conversations Just for Women.*"

- Jami

"*Difficult Conversations Just for Women* gave me tips, tools and techniques that can be utilized everyday to keep my mindset maximized. Backed by studies and statistics, this entertaining read will come off the bookshelf time and again."

- Debbie

"Written in a practical, relatable (and funny!) manner, *Difficult Conversations Just for Women* lays out a communication blueprint that anyone can follow. Using the No Fear approach, I was able to change an uncomfortable situation with a neighbor from a stalemate to a win-win!'

- Mary

"As a former International Human Resources Specialist with over ten years of corporate and vendor global mobility experience, all I can say when reading *Difficult Conversations Just For Women* is, "This is a must-read! Where was this book during my time in the corporate world?

This book provides the much needed "breath of fresh air" in addressing difficult relationships. It provides hope that with this new approach of Wiki-Women those damaging relationships which used to define our professional and personal lives will be a thing of the past."

- Missy

Santiago, Sofia,
Difficult conversations
just for women : kill t
[2016]
33305236966523
sa   10/21/16

Difficult

Conversations

Just for Women

KILL THE ANXIETY. GET WHAT YOU WANT.

Sofia Santiago, MBA, PMP

Dr. Susan Harrison

Difficult Conversations *Just for Women*: Kill the Anxiety. Get What You Want.
By Sofia Santiago, MBA, PMP and Dr. Susan Harrison

All rights reserved. No part of this book may be reproduced or transmitted in any form or by any means, electronic or mechanical, including photocopying, recording or by any information storage and retrieval system, without written permission from the authors, except for the inclusion of brief quotations in a review.

Copyright © 2016 by The WikiWomen Academy, a division of WikiWorkshops, LLC.
Cover Illustration Copyright © 2016 by The WikiWomen Academy.
Design contributors: Dani De la Chica and Jordan Harrison.

ISBN-10: 1533546983; ISBN-13: 978-1533546982

The WikiWomen Academy, a division of WikiWorkshops, LLC. Overland Park, Kansas.

WikiWomen is a trademark of WikiWorkshops. All trademarks belong to their respective owners. All quotes are used with permission of the copyright owner(s) or under fair use principles. Unattributed quotations are by the authors.

ORDERING INFORMATION

For information on keynotes, workshops, volume discounts, and bulk orders please contact us through our website:

www.TheWikiWomenAcademy.com

DISCLAIMERS. This work is provided "as is." The authors and publisher (A&P) make no guarantees or warranties as to the accuracy, adequacy or completeness of or results to be obtained from using the advice in this book, and expressly disclaim any warranty, express or implied, including but not limited to implied warranties of fitness for a particular purpose. The A&P does not warrant or guarantee that the functions contained in the work will meet your requirements or that it will be error free. Although the A&P has made every effort to ensure that the information in this book is correct, they do not assume and hereby disclaim any liability to any party for any loss, damage, or disruption caused by errors or omissions, regardless of their cause. To maintain their anonymity, we have changed the names of individuals and places. This book is sold with the understanding that the A&P are not engaged in rendering legal, psychological, or any other professional service. If expert assistance is required, the services of a competent professional person should be sought.

To all WikiWomen™

WikiWoman™

/ˈwikeˈwoomən/

noun

A wiki is a website that allows collaborative modification of its content: everyone contributes and everyone benefits.

A WikiWoman chooses to collaborate with other women rather than to compete with them.

A WikiWoman is a woman who learns, grows, and improves every area of her life while helping other women to do the same.

Everyone contributes and everyone benefits.

CONTENTS

Introduction **11**

CHAPTER 1
Difficult Conversations 101 **25**

CHAPTER 2
Fears and Worries **35**

CHAPTER 3
Do This *Before* the Difficult Conversation **63**

CHAPTER 4
The NO FEAR™ Method **95**

CHAPTER 5
The Must-Have Elements of Your Conversation **111**

CHAPTER 6
What to Do *During* the Difficult Conversation **121**

CHAPTER 7
Keep Your Emotions Under Control **145**

CHAPTER 8
What *Not* to Do *During* the Difficult Conversation **169**

CHAPTER 9
What to Do *After* the Difficult Conversation **193**

One Last Word **203**

References **205**

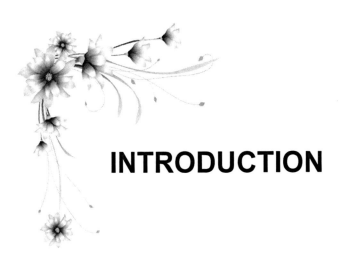

INTRODUCTION

What will you do this upcoming October 23? I ask only because it's a national holiday most people don't know about, but many would celebrate it if they did.

October 23 is National Slap Your Irritating Co-worker Day.

We actually don't suggest using that day as an excuse to avoid handling a difficult conversation. Perhaps you've been avoiding one with that arrogant new hire that interrupts you all the time, or with the woman that follows you from the elevator to your desk on Monday mornings gossiping non-stop about everyone else in the office. And what about the man that you've caught twice with his feet on your desk (while you were at lunch), clipping his nails and leaving your floor all sprinkled with his DNA? (Eek!) Is your boss included? Then this might be your chance to make her pay for all the times she has yelled at you, or scared you into tears. And what about your husband? Since you both take care of work at home, does he count as a co-worker too?

But wait! Just in case you think you want to use the holiday as an excuse to slap your irritating co-worker, hang on. Let me introduce you to a few women who may remind you of someone you care about—maybe even yourself. After meeting them you may change your mind and decide to handle things differently.

Meet Sofia, a Tough Cookie

About ten years ago I spent a three-month vacation in an all-inclusive exotic place I never thought I'd ever visit, where I met people I thought I'd never meet, and where I did things I thought I'd never do. A battered women's shelter in Texas.

My (back then) soon-to-be-ex had frozen my credit cards and bank accounts and my manager had assigned all my hard earned clients to other financial advisors. This was the right thing to do, since the stock market doesn't wait and neither should clients. So I was thrilled when an opportunity came up for me to apply for a new job in another state (I needed to move for safety reasons anyway).

I left my little daughter with the administrative assistant at my former job and flew to Missouri for a day packed with interviews. I had sixteen. Plus, I had to do a demonstration of my coaching skills and a presentation to a group of about ten people who would assess my training skills.

When I was a size zero my self-esteem was even smaller than my body (have you heard of the shelter diet?), but I still managed to nail the interviews. My soon-to-be-boss walked me to the door and when I asked him what my chances were he replied, "I'm not sure, because you are Hispanic, and Hispanic women are submissive. I don't know if you'll be able to handle a group of 60 type-A personality males every month." (I was not applying for a zookeeper job—just as a sales trainer to financial advisors.)

When I heard that, I was speechless. By the time I thought of asking him, "Well, doesn't my background of owning a successful training company for over 15 years count?" he had already turned and walked away. Little did I know then that this had been a turning point in my life.

Despite his comments, I was hired. And although I loved my job, I resented what my boss said. "How dare he?" I would tell myself. To prove him wrong I became as tough as could be. I was going to show him—and the rest of the world—that I was not a submissive Latina. No sir.

"To succeed in the world of men," I told myself, "I'll just behave like them." (I promised myself I would still use the ladies room and never scratch weird places in public though.)

Picture me walking to my office confidently, wearing a wide smile, playing in my mind the song *There's a New Man in Town* (YouTube it), thinking that if guys were tough and got away with what they wanted, I would too—I'd do what they did. Why not? If I had once become a bicultural Hispanic-American, now I could become tri-cultural woman-man.

So I started being direct and aggressive. I faced difficult conversations head on. When I felt someone was stepping on me I'd confront him on the spot, even when it wasn't a big deal. (I guess all those years of being stepped on were finally over for good.) That's how I became a "too tough" of a tough cookie. If someone cut me off in line (especially if it was a tall man) I didn't wait to find out if it had been by mistake—I'd tap him on the shoulder and sustaining eye contact I'd say, "Excuse me, the line is back there." I know that if Susan (my co-author and business partner) had known me back then she would have thought, "Are you serious? Did you really do that?" (You'll meet Susan in the next section and you'll see what I mean.)

Knowing that women are interrupted about three times as much as men,[1] when someone talked over me in a meeting I'd make a stop sign with my hand and say "I'm not finished," and would keep talking, instead of acting like the other (sweet) girls did. Does this sound "witchy" too you? It certainly didn't seem that way to me. Back then aggressive and assertive were the same to me.

Did I miss any good opportunities for that reason? I don't know. Back then I didn't know:

1. Women that are aggressive are not usually liked as much.
2. Being liked is (almost) a must for career advancement.
3. Therefore, being aggressive harms a woman's career in ways she may not even be aware of.[2]

Research suggests that when someone does not conform to stereotyped roles, he or she is penalized through social rejection,[3] and being aggressive is considered masculine.

Women who value authenticity and directness can be judged unfairly[4] (unless you're over 95 or look like Halle Berry).

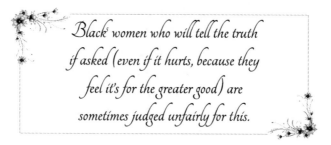

Black women who will tell the truth if asked (even if it hurts, because they feel it's for the greater good) are sometimes judged unfairly for this.

Black women also tend to value the open expression of their opinions,[6] and this may have negative effects.

Outsiders often perceive this style of communication as intense, outspoken, challenging, and confrontational, and when this assertive style is used, Black American women are often perceived as argumentative and dominant, forceful and aggressive.[7]

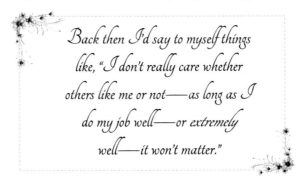

Back then I'd say to myself things like, "I don't really care whether others like me or not—as long as I do my job well—or extremely well—it won't matter."

Little did I know that being liked matters *a lot* in business (and in life). The more well liked you are, the more likely you are to keep your job, the more respect and recognition you'll get, the more support you'll have from others, and the more successful you'll be.[8] Research also shows:

Not being liked can negatively impact women's work relationships, access to social networks, day-to-day interactions and, ultimately, their advancement opportunities.[9]

I can't tell you the opportunities I missed for not being liked enough because nobody was going to tell me, "We didn't pick you for this project because you're a bit of a witch." Of course not— there would always be a "valid" reason.

Once I understood those unspoken rules, I knew something needed to change. Very likely, ME.

As a recent immigrant and a new hire there were three things I had yet to learn in order to survive:

1. First, how to communicate in order to be perceived neither too soft nor too tough (as women are[10]) but just right.
2. Second, how to control my emotions so I wouldn't revert to being aggressive when things heated up during a difficult conversation.
3. The third thing I needed to learn to survive was, "Where's the cafeteria?"

I started doing what every reasonable introvert does to learn about the world: I read. I learned and taught, and I taught and learned. Fast forward and I have read tons of books, completed half a graduate degree in intercultural communication, and held hundreds of conversations with the women who have attended my *Just for Women* workshops. That's when I met Dr. Susan Harrison and this book was born.

Meet Susan, The Sweetie Pie

Sometimes I think that I became a people pleaser because of the rewards I got from it—acceptance, validation, belonging, love—all those good feelings I craved.

The technical name is *operant conditioning*. You may have heard it: It means that when you get rewarded for behaving in a certain way you're likely to repeat that behavior. My people pleasing seemed to get me the rewards I felt I needed.

I was, like many of you, raised as a *nice* girl. I learned from an early age to be a giver rather than a taker. And I'm proud of that—I just don't remember when or why I started putting other people's needs so far above mine that I somehow buried the care for my own *self* too deep.

I wanted everyone to like me. No, I *needed* people to like me. I said yes a lot and overcommitted myself and then I'd have to cancel on someone—which doesn't feel good, especially for a people pleaser. I also said *yes* to people even when I wanted to say *no*.

I seldom asked for what I wanted or stated what I needed. Had I considered the possibility of having a difficult conversation I would have avoided it—but the truth is that it almost never crossed my mind.

We often think, "Who am I to ask for something special? I'll just make do."

Although I have a lot of examples of wanting to be liked, the following is perhaps the most pitiful: When I was driving and it sprinkled I would look around at other cars to see if they were using their windshield wipers. I wouldn't use mine unless they were using theirs or else I was sure they'd think I was stupid. My fear was that they wouldn't like me.

Seriously. That was my life. Throughout my travels I have told that story to many women. I was actually shocked to find out how many of them had not only acted irrationally in order for people to like them, but many had done the same thing with the windshield wipers!

With all of my people pleasing, I became "too sweet" of a sweetie pie. And, you may recognize this: I was called "too nice" and believe me, that isn't usually a compliment.

I remember an occasion when I had to travel to another state to speak at a conference. I have a mild case of claustrophobia, which I discovered when we tried to fit a ton of girls into a Volkswagen, in college (that's another story!) Due to my claustrophobia, I prefer the aisle seat and this time was no exception. However, I didn't realize until it was too late that I had been assigned a window seat.

To make matters worse, this was a tiny plane and my row was the last row and it didn't even have a window. When I got to my place there was a woman already on the aisle seat. For a split second I considered asking her to switch with me—but I couldn't. I could not get myself to ask her because I just "knew" she would say no. Then the flight was delayed but we had already boarded. We sat on the tarmac for over 45 minutes. As I sat there the panic began to set in and I felt everything closing in on me. After about 15 minutes, the plane went dark (except for those little lights on the floor) and the air went off. I was close to screaming but held it in tightly.

If Sofia had known me back then she would have said, "Are you serious? You went through all that and didn't ask her to switch?" And, I know she would have been right! Even as I type this I still feel a bit of the panic I felt in that moment. And to think, I could have prevented it all if I would have not avoided a potentially difficult conversation.

When people hear the words *difficult conversation* they probably think of making an intimate request to a spouse without hurting his feelings, or asking a rude boss to stop micromanaging without seeming bossy. But for me even the most basic requests were often difficult.

One day I decided I was tired of all the stress that I was causing myself. Here's what happened. Unbeknownst to her, it was my sister Kathy who made me realize that my people pleasing was hurting others more than helping them. One day she invited me out to lunch with her and my niece. We went to lunch often, but there were plenty of times when I changed my plans and cancelled because someone else needed me and I knew I could go out to lunch with them another time. This day was one of those times.

When I told her I couldn't make it, she replied, "Oh, that's okay." She didn't even seem disappointed this time. Later I asked her if my niece was okay and she replied in a nice tone without any sarcasm, "I told Morgan that sometimes you can't count on Aunt Susie to do what she says she will do." Oh my goodness, that broke my heart and ended up being the catalyst I needed and she didn't even know the impact she was making. She was just matter-of-factly explaining what she told her daughter.

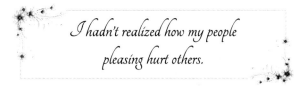

I hadn't realized how my people pleasing hurt others.

I was trying so hard to please everyone that I was pleasing no one and I was disappointing those I cared about the most!

That's where my journey of self-improvement started. Over the years I've met many other women who were just like me. Research actually shows that as women we tend not to ask for what we want and need, and we pay handsomely for this, financially and otherwise. For instance, not negotiating a salary offer can cost a woman as much as three-quarters of a million dollars over her working lifetime.[11] (I could use some of that now!)

Little by little I figured out what I needed to do in order to change. These things included:

1. Pinpoint my fears and start the process of controlling them.
2. Learn how to start a difficult conversation. I just didn't know how to start or which words to use!
3. Learn what to do when the other person wanted to take control of the conversation or interrupted me.
4. Learn how to stop apologizing and using weak language.

In summation, I needed to become "assertive." But you may be asking, what exactly does that mean anyway? As a part of my journey, I did some research and learned when people refer to you as assertive it generally means you exhibit confidence, you can speak up and stand up for yourself, you have no problem asking for what you want, you feel comfortable disagreeing with someone, you speak directly, and you use "I" statements, which means you are not accusatory but responsible for your behaviors. (If you read that as fast as I wrote it, breathe.)

Interestingly enough, studies show that many times women are penalized for being assertive, especially by older men,[12] and cultural stereotypes affect women from certain ethnic groups more than others. For instance, when examining the barriers to success for Asian American women, attorney Peggy Li explains:

> *The perception of Asian women in the nineteenth century as sexual objects, and the perception of Asian Americans in the twentieth century as model minorities permeate our conception of Asian American women today. Generally, Asian Americans are perceived to be overly competent, yet not warm, sociable, aggressive, or assertive.*[13]

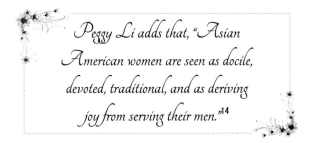

Peggy Li adds that, "Asian American women are seen as docile, devoted, traditional, and as deriving joy from serving their men."[14]

Besides being a style of responding, assertiveness has been thought to be a personality trait—this would mean that some people are inherently more assertive than others. Studying this, I learned that there's some evidence that extroverts tend to be social, gregarious, dominant, ambitious, and—you guessed it— assertive.[15] "I'm an extrovert, so what happened?" I was wondering, when I read about another personality trait: *agreeableness*. Uh-oh.

Agreeable people are cooperative (trusting, caring) and likeable (good natured, gentle). They also are soft-hearted and tolerant.[16]

And—non-assertive. Goodness! That sounded awfully familiar. But despite the complications, my story has a good ending. After that first step I gradually started gaining more and more confidence in myself, and that's how I eventually learned what I now know.

I've come a long way. People even compliment me on being able to stand up for myself and I get asked for advice on it regularly. What a difference! I became assertive and you can too. However, that doesn't mean I'm never afraid or nervous before standing up for myself. You may never get rid of your fears, and that's okay, but the same way some martial art practitioners use the strength and energy in their own body and direct it towards their target, you can learn how to use your fears as energy that propels you to stand up for yourself, just like I did.

Fast forward about twenty years from when my journey began, after having conversations with thousands of other women, personally and professionally, I met Sofia Santiago and together we became WikiWomen and this book was born.

Meet Mary Jo, Suzanne, and Sam

Once upon a time there was a woman named Mary Jo Cook. She was an ambitious executive who was in a bind because she wanted to spend time with her young daughter without slowing down her career development. (We're sure many of you have been there.)

Mary Jo designed a new position for herself and negotiated a new schedule. When the scope of the job became too much, Mary Jo and her colleague Suzanne Hengelmann, who was also an executive and a mom, decided to share the role.

What's wonderful and unique about their story is how they did it: these two women not only shared responsibilities, but they merged themselves into one entity.

Each worked three days a week, overlapping on Wednesdays. They shared a title (vice president), a voicemail, and an email account. They even went by a joint name, Sam, a combination of Suzanne and MJ.[17]

Meet the WikiWomen

We, Sofia and Susan, found Sam's collaboration so inspiring, that we decided to blend our experience and start a *movement*. We called it *WikiWomen*.

A *wiki* is a website that allows *collaborative* modification of its content and structure. Just like Wikipedia, for instance, where anyone may contribute, everyone brings something to the table, and everyone benefits. You don't need to be an expert to contribute—all you need is willingness (and maybe even passion) to share. As you share, you become part of a community.

With that model in mind we created *WikiWomen*. A Wiki Woman is a woman who wants to learn, grow, and improve every area of her life while helping other women to do the same. We envisioned an ever-growing community where professional women from all walks of life, colors and flavors could collaborate and help each other develop the skills they need to succeed in business and in life.

We launched *WikiWomen* as a Meetup® group on January 27 of 2016. Meetup.com is a website that allows anyone to organize a local group or find one to join. We stated our vision and scheduled several *WikiWednesdays*. Approximately every other Wednesday evening we meet at a restaurant in the Overland Park, Kansas, area to learn from an expert in her field, a professional speaker, or a mover and shaker in our community. *WikiWomen* offers high-caliber speakers *for free*, and lets women focus on learning in a relaxed environment. Speakers donate their time to contribute to our mission.

Professional women heard our message loud and clear. In less than a week we had almost one hundred members, and for our first-ever conference we had a full house. Within two days our second scheduled conference was booked and women were signing up for the waiting list. Women were rating our group with five stars, inviting their friends, and even donating money into our account, without having been asked. Just because they wanted to collaborate.

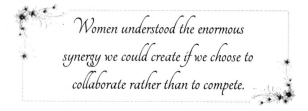

Women understood the enormous synergy we could create if we choose to collaborate rather than to compete.

Over the following weeks we heard several wikiwomen ask us about their specific circumstances, and share with us their success stories using the NO FEAR™ model you will learn here. That's why we, the founders of *WikiWomen*, decided to spread our wings and bring our secrets to many more women. We created *The WikiWomen Academy for the Development of Professional Women* to promote our initiative of women collaborating to improve themselves through education.

We also decided to blend both our writing-selves into one voice to write *The WikiWomen's Wisdom* series of books. That's why you'll see most of it written with "I" and no differentiation of whom is speaking. You are holding the first wikibook in your hands. We've been playing "ping-pong-writing" to compile our knowledge and stories about how the strategies that work for men don't necessarily help women, and about how women can navigate difficult conversations more successfully.

With our combined voice we want to have a one-on-one conversation and share our secrets with you. Just like good friends do. Enjoy!

Sofia & Susan

CHAPTER ONE

DIFFICULT CONVERSATIONS 101

"*My* friend Tulip and her husband Crispin were having a great time at a water park last summer. Suddenly, Crispin saw a woman who seemed to be having a blast, jumping up and down, laughing, and having a great time in the water. Only she had lost the top of her bikini."

That's how I usually start my conference on difficult conversations. At this point I pause and enjoy looking at the audience's reaction. When I'm telling this story to a group of women they gasp empathetically. In mixed groups men grin.

Dumbfounded by his discovery, Crispin did what any intelligent man would do: he went to ask his wife for direction. Talk about needing to know how to deal with a difficult conversation! Tulip said, "That woman will eventually figure it out on her own." End of story. But then both of them kept an eye on that woman. Perhaps Crispin kept two.

Then the waves stopped, the woman came out of the pool, and they could see clearly that "she" was a man!

Can you imagine what could have happened if Crispin had decided to go have that difficult conversation? Hopefully he would have observed the truth of the matter before it was too late.

When I heard this story I couldn't believe it! Still, here is my point: observing and getting our facts straight before having a difficult conversation is key. And it's one of the steps we need to follow when preparing. But I'm getting ahead of myself. Let's start by defining what we understand as a difficult conversation.

What is a Difficult Conversation?

Actually, the story with which we started this chapter is more about jumping to conclusions than about having to face a difficult conversation. It's only difficult because the topic is sexual in nature, and that makes it a delicate issue and embarrassing to handle. Had she lost one of her earrings instead, it would have been easy to go and tell her. And maybe even help her to search for it.

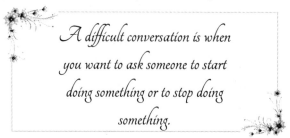

A difficult conversation is when you want to ask someone to start doing something or to stop doing something.

A difficult conversation is normally not difficult due to embarrassment, but because you're asking someone else to change.

Here are a few examples of the type of difficult situations we will be discussing:

- You want one of your co-workers to *stop* interrupting and talking over you during meetings.
- You want your supervisor to *stop* reprimanding you in public.
- You want your co-worker to *stop* gossiping about you behind your back.
- You want your mother-in-law to *start* calling before she shows up.
- You want your husband to *start* doing the dishes.

Why Have a Difficult Conversation?

There are valid reasons behind difficult conversations. There are instances when you need to have one in order to preserve your dignity or your well-being as well as that of others.

Here are some of those instances:

- When someone has invaded, alienated, or disrespected your rights and you need to stand up for yourself.
- When the other person has a negative attitude, a closed mind, uncontrolled anger, a positional stance, or any other barrier to an amicable agreement.
- When there's something you want or need from someone you love in order to improve the relationship.

- When someone you love is displaying a self-destructive behavior and you can assist him, for instance, by getting him professional help.

Most often, you need to speak up when someone offends you. Offenses fall into four categories:[1]

1. Relational (e.g. insulting someone)
2. Failed obligation (e.g. failing to complete chores)
3. Inconvenience (e.g. calling a wrong number)
4. Physical or material (e.g. bumping into someone, damaging someone's belongings)

Some other times, even when there was no offense, having a difficult conversation may be what it takes to improve your quality of life or relationship.

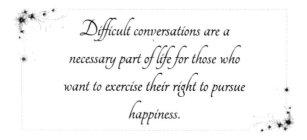

Difficult conversations are a necessary part of life for those who want to exercise their right to pursue happiness.

How Women Approach Difficult Conversations

Years ago, when I was in restaurant management, we had one female server who smelled really bad. One night a few managers were talking about this girl and how she smelled but no one wanted to tell her. I couldn't take it and I said, "I will talk to her."

A few minutes later I took her outside to the back of the restaurant for privacy (and open air!) I was so scared to have this conversation and I didn't know how to start it. But I just started talking and blurted out, "When I am around you sometimes I smell an odor."

Then the girl said, "Sometimes I go to my dad's farm before work and I probably am stepping in something."

I smiled and said, "I bet that's it," but I was thinking "That ain't it." I didn't know what else to say at that point. The next week the girl came back to work and she didn't smell bad, so even though I did not have a perfect conversation I still got the results I wanted.

I know that women tend to shy away from difficult conversations. Unless they're cornered. (Keep in mind we are generalizing. Take what fits you.) And when they do they tend to ramble, speak indirectly, chicken out at the last minute by changing the subject, or leave without having said exactly what they want.

Then, when the other person doesn't change because he didn't even understand what it was that we were asking of him, we feel rejected, resent him and find consolation in telling someone else about it.

Many factors determine how we communicate (our gender, personality, ethnic group, generation, experiences, etc.) Still, most women prefer to avoid head-on difficult conversations.

Why Women Approach Difficult Conversations Differently Than Men

Many studies have tried to explain why men and women approach difficult conversations differently. Researchers have found all kinds of reasons: biological, genetic, cultural, social, moral, etc.

Let's start with the biological ones. Did you know that our biology explains (at least in part) why we react to stressors differently than men? You've heard about the fight-or-flight response, right? You know, the physiological changes that occur in our body when we perceive an attack or any threat to our survival: we release hormones that prepare our body to either stay and deal with the threat or to run away to safety.

Picture this: a caveman (think Geico®) sees a sabre-toothed tiger rapidly approaching. If he's with his buddies and has a few spears (or has liquid courage) he may decide to face the beast. If not, he'll run as fast as he can.

Now picture a female version of that Geico® caveman. The cavewoman, when first spotting the approaching sabre-toothed cat, instead of fighting it or fleeing, goes to find her girlfriend, tells her about the huge animal, and hugs her. How does that make sense? Well, that's why this is so fascinating: when facing a threat, women's bodies activate certain hormones that *dampen* the effects of the fight-or-flight system.[6] This seems to be a strategy designed to protect the offspring.

Dr. Craske, professor of psychology, psychiatry and bio behavioral sciences at the University of California, Los Angeles (UCLA) explains it this way:

Instead of fighting or fleeing, a woman's drive during stress is to tend to her children and befriend others for the security of group protection. Importantly, this natural tend-and-befriend stress response may reinforce an avoidant way of coping with perceived threats, which can ultimately reinforce anxiety and the perception of threat.

It does make sense when we think that a cavewoman won't flee (leaving her babies unprotected) or fight (leaving her babies as potential orphans) but instead will look for the security of group protection (for her and for her kids).

This might explain why, when the boss informs employees of an upcoming "restructure" (a.k.a. downsizing), while men may start applying for other jobs or go talk to the boss to clarify why they should be the ones to keep their jobs, a female worker might discuss the situation with other female co-workers. And feel even more stressed about the situation.

Although men's fight-or-flight response exposes them to more threats, it also gives them the chance to find effective ways of defeating those threats. This is another way that men learn independence and assertiveness.

No wonder I haven't seen any workshop on assertiveness skills *just for men.*

But the reasons why women and men approach difficult conversations differently are not only biological. Boys and girls are raised differently, and that matters. One of the reasons offered to explain why women avoid difficult conversations is we've been raised not to say things to others that might make them feel bad. "If you don't have something nice to say ..."

Deborah Tannen, Ph.D. professor of linguistics at Georgetown University in Washington, D.C., explains it is as if we have an inner censor that stops our tongue—or twists it—so we communicate potentially hurtful information in ways that many others miss entirely.[2]

We may not even be aware of how the assumptions that worked for us when we were little girls playing with other girls don't fly in a workplace where the rules that men set decades ago still determine who succeeds and who doesn't.

One of those assumptions, for instance, is that since you treat others with courtesy you can safely assume others will give you the respect you deserve.

> *Boys . . . learn to use language to challenge one another and deflect challenges as a way of negotiating status in a group. In fact, boys often use confrontation for fun, by mock-arguing, teasing, or play fighting. In this spirit, many men assume they have to demand respect or others will see weakness.*[3]

The Girl Scouts of USA and Sheryl Sandberg, COO of Facebook, co-creators of the Ban Bossy campaign to eliminate the word bossy from the English language because of its harmful effect on girls, explain:

> *When a little boy asserts himself, he's called a "leader." Yet when a little girl does the same, she risks being branded "bossy." Words like bossy send a message: don't raise your hand or speak up.*[4]

Biological, educational—there are even moral explanations as to why women and men approach difficult conversations differently. For instance, Kohlberg, who established a theory of *moral development* based on reasoning about justice, describes women's desire to preserve relationships and to live up to the expectations of others, and contrasts it with men's desire for law and order where the laws have to be upheld to maintain social order.[5]

My point is this: for the reasons stated previously (and many more), women need to *learn* and re-learn different strategies to ask for and get what they want.

Think of What You May Be Missing

I'll leave you with a last thought: when you avoid a difficult conversation, you're missing something. If you're not happy, telling your friends about it instead of talking to the person is a mistake. You may think that talking about it will ease your pain, but it doesn't. You need the pain to be gone and dealing with the other person is the fastest way to make that happen.

Another mistake is giving the silent treatment. Being silent is an offense to the other party—you're not giving him the opportunity to make things better. You are placing the burden on him to be a mind reader. And you may build resentment against him unfairly because he didn't have the chance to explain. This behavior is passive aggressive.

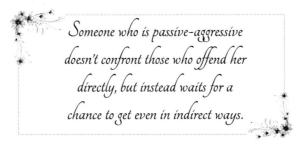

Someone who is passive-aggressive doesn't confront those who offend her directly, but instead waits for a chance to get even in indirect ways.

On a few occasions I've had a workshop evaluation that reads something like, "The room was too hot." I feel sorry for the woman that spent the whole day participating in a workshop in a room that was too hot for her instead of speaking up. As the workshop leader I could have done something about it had I known. But she deprived me of the opportunity to serve her. I know life is not fair, but the point is that not speaking up is usually a proposition where everyone loses.

> *You'll never know what you're missing when avoiding difficult conversations, but I can assure you, you're missing something.*

What Did You Learn?

This is a good time to stop and reflect. Take some time to process what you read. Perhaps you'll want to start a journal and write a few notes. Don't censor yourself—this is for your eyes only. Think about one or two situations that have been bothering you. Do any of them call for you to ask someone to change their behavior? Do any of them require you to plan on having a difficult conversation? Why have you been avoiding those particular conversations?

CHAPTER TWO

FEARS AND WORRIES

*T*he fact you are reading this book tells me that there's a difficult conversation you've been avoiding (or you are my mom.) Well, here's the first thing you need to know: before you confront the other party, you need to prepare thoroughly, and the first step in preparing is to face your fears and worries, so let's get you ready.

Why devote a whole chapter to fears and worries? Two reasons.

1. Unless you acknowledge your fears and work on controlling them, they will control you throughout the difficult conversation.
2. Women tend to struggle more with anxiety and worry than men.

> *Women are twice as likely as men to develop anxiety disorders.*

Before going any further let us clarify for those of you who are language purists (like one of us—the one who refuses to confess it's her) what we'll talk about in this section are *anxieties*, not *fears*. Technically, *fear* is what you feel in the presence of a clear and identifiable threat (you're in trouble!), whereas anxiety occurs in the absence of danger.

Anxiety is the discomfort you feel when you have a sense of dread, even when you're not in danger.[3] And then *worry* is what you say to yourself when you're anxious, usually in anticipation of some future outcome or event.[4]

Let's say, this morning your Yorkie escaped from your arms and ran away, and you saw a large dog running towards her. You were genuinely afraid. Later, at the office, you're still finishing a report that was due *yesterday*, when you see your boss rapidly approaching your office. Your boss looks unhappy, so you start getting anxious. Both situations are stressful, but there's a difference: in one of them you're facing a dangerous creature that can cause a lot of harm; in the other you're just facing a dog. Kidding. But you see the difference, right? I certainly hope so!

Throughout this book we'll use the words fear, anxiety, and worry interchangeably, based on common usage. (For instance, you've heard of *fear of rejection*, but not of *anxiety of rejection*.). That being said, let's go back to talking about the fears you may feel at the possibility of a confrontation.

Women's tendency to struggle with anxiety and worry more than men has been studied by Dr. Michelle Craske, Director of the UCLA Anxiety Disorders Behavioral Research Program.[1] According to Dr. Craske some of the possible explanations for these phenomena are differences in how boys and girls are raised, women's natural tendency to experience certain emotions more intensely than men, and even biological differences in how women and men respond to stress.[2]

So the first thing you need to do when preparing for a difficult conversation is this: cut yourself some slack.

> *Don't be too hard on yourself, and—above all—don't worry about worrying too much.*

Besides that, you need to acknowledge that in the big scheme of things your problem is really not that big. Okay, so it feels big, but just remind yourself that nobody is going to die as a result of this difficult conversation. When you realize that, you'll be on your way toward building up the strength and confidence needed to take the risk.

> *Let the wisdom of a great woman, Eleanor Roosevelt, inspire you. She said, "You gain strength, courage and confidence by every experience in which you really stop to look fear in the face."*

If you suspect you're rationalizing your fears by telling yourself things such as, "Why bother, if I already know what she's going to say?" "It's really not that important," "I don't want to hurt his feelings," or "I know that over time this problem will go away," you need to stop and ask yourself, "What am I afraid of?"

So, What Are You Afraid Of?

Some experts list these ten people's top fears of facing conflict:[5]

1. Fear of harm
2. Fear of rejection
3. Fear of loss of a relationship
4. Fear of anger
5. Fear of saying the wrong thing
6. Fear of being seen as selfish
7. Fear of failing
8. Fear of hurting someone else
9. Fear of getting what you want
10. Fear of intimacy
11. Fear of not being liked
12. Fear of being considered too aggressive (or a "witch")

Yeah, that's 12. We added the last two because they're particularly relevant to women.

Let's break down these fears. As you read about each of them ask yourself if it may be affecting you.

Fear of Harm

This person may be able to harm you in some way. This could even be a fear of physical harm. This is truly a fear, not just a worry.

Being in real danger is the right reason to avoid confronting someone and, instead, focus on finding alternative solutions to the problem. You probably want to call the police to stop a burglar instead of using the NO FEAR™ method on him!

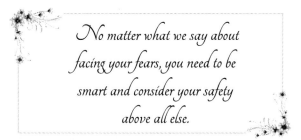

No matter what we say about facing your fears, you need to be smart and consider your safety above all else.

If you're dealing with a volatile person, make sure you're not alone. In fact, we recommend having the conversation in a public place, if at all.

Perhaps you are afraid of retaliation. Definitely document the place, date, time, and what was discussed. This is for your protection if something negative does happen. The majority of the time if you prepare well and have the right attitude, a poor outcome is less likely; however, be prepared.

Fear of Rejection

I'm not blonde. Did you know that some men will only date blondes? I'm sure there are men that also only date women with mustaches, but who am I to judge? The point is that I have felt rejected over things I couldn't really control and I've been rejected over things I could control. Who cares? We will all be rejected and it happens more than we probably even know about.

You might feel rejected and the other person might actually be rejecting you in some manner. Even if they just don't agree, you can feel rejected. Get over it. Wow! That does sound harsh.

> *The truth is not everyone is going to agree with you and some will reject you, and that's okay.*

Now say it. "Some people will reject me and it's okay." You may still need to have the difficult conversation.

Have you considered they may not be rejecting you, but an idea you presented, or the implications of a request you made? We'll talk about not taking things personally later. For now, just think that if they do, chances are they'll use the word *no*, so let's talk about that particular word.

Make the Word "No" Your Friend

In America, the word *no* tends to mean *no*, because Americans value clear and direct communication. However, in the multicultural world we live in, *no* doesn't mean the same thing to all people. In many countries, the idea of "No" is not always so clear cut, and since it depends on the context and culture, it may have other meanings, such as, "Keep trying to convince me and we'll see."

The word *no* has nuances based on gender and how it's spoken. Cynthia, in our WikiWomen group, told me once

Men seem to be at an advantage in that they're genetically engineered to turn a women's "No" into a "Yes." It becomes

the art of persuasion and can pay great dividends in their career when they want their idea to be accepted in a staff meeting or a prospective client's business. It's an offensive tactic or maneuver they may not even be conscious of.

So stop fearing the word *no*. Next time you get one, start by understanding it's not an absolute, irrefutable, non-negotiable, written in stone answer. It may mean "Maybe," or "I might be persuaded," or "Tweak your request and I'll re-evaluate it," or even "Not at this time."

Remember in the introduction I said studies show that women don't make enough requests for themselves? Well, why not ask the person who said "No" for more "intelligence," by asking questions such as these:

- "What can I do to turn that *no* into a *yes*?"

- "Under which circumstances should I ask again to increase my chances of getting a *yes*?"

- "How would my request need to be different to get a *yes*?"

- "*No*? Tell me more, please."

You are creative, I know, so just get over the self-limiting beliefs that tell you that once you get your first "No" the game is over. Remember Yogi Berra, the famous baseball player and coach: "It's not over until it's over." Armed with new information, do what most men do: go back to your office and come up with a way to turn that "No" into a "Yes" by changing the conditions of your question or proposal.

You know the saying, "The best time to plant a tree was 20 years ago. The second best time is right now," so commit to stop fearing the big bad "No" today!

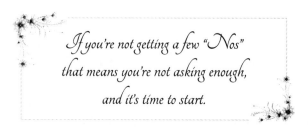

If you're not getting a few "Nos"
that means you're not asking enough,
and it's time to start.

Fear of Loss of a Relationship

Losing a relationship can be scary. Oh my goodness. I can speak to this one. In order not to lose a relationship, I allowed so many unhealthy things to happen. I was more concerned about losing the relationship than I was respecting myself and I paid dearly. My health suffered, my self-esteem suffered and I lost the relationship anyway.

Of course, you want to choose your battles and not bring up everything, but studies have found that couples who are inclined to avoid conflict are less satisfied with their marriages than couples who confront conflicts.[6]

Fear of Anger

It is okay if someone is angry with you. I think this one reverts back to childhood (maybe they all do) because most of us didn't want our parents mad at us. We were sensitive to people being upset. Maybe I'm just talking about myself here! Regardless, this doesn't have to be your issue.

Let the other person be mad if it means that you can't have a difficult conversation without her getting mad. Please! Isn't it really her problem at that point?

You handle the conversation as well as you can and maintain *your* composure. If she gets angry and you need to leave before finishing all the steps, leave and address it at another time. Or if you tend to become angry in response to the comments that she makes to the point you can't continue rationally, come back another time.

> *Everyone needs to deal with their own emotions. Don't get sucked into being overly responsible for others' emotions.*

Fear of Saying the Wrong Thing

I used to work with the youth at my church. One night I was taking a girl home and she was eating powdered doughnuts, and the white powder got all over her clothes and hands. I made a joke about her doing cocaine, and we started laughing so hard we could hardly control ourselves. For some reason we found it insanely funny. But you may not be surprised to know that the parents did not find it funny. The parents called me and told me that doing drugs is nothing to joke about. I was so afraid of saying the wrong thing back to them that I decided not to say much, except apologize.

Are you afraid of saying the wrong thing? Sometimes you will make a mistake. And guess what? It is okay. (Sensing a theme here?) Scripting ahead of time helps prevent this but sometimes you don't have the chance to script.

Each time, think it over so you are less likely to repeat past errors. Then learn from them and go on because it will not be the last time. All we can do is improve. That also means don't beat yourself up. I have said so many things that seemed wrong to others! I could continually beat myself up over them, but I don't. When they come to mind I simply say, "That's over. I can't fix it and now all I can do is not repeat it."

Fear of Being Seen as Selfish

I care about the environment but I will not take my showers only when the rain comes. Does that make me selfish? Maybe to someone. Ever hidden a candy bar from your children and then ate it when they weren't around? Me too! Aren't we selfish?

My friends and I like to joke about being selfish, and say things such as, "It's all about me." And, "I'm sorry, did you not understand this is about what I want?" Well, the truth is that difficult conversations are for your own sanity.

They are for your peace of mind and they are about your rights. But, they are also about the relationship itself, and they benefit both parties when they are handled in a healthy and respectful manner.

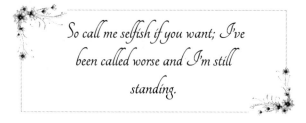

So call me selfish if you want; I've been called worse and I'm still standing.

Fear of Failing

Could fear of failure be the reason women tend to be more conservative with investments in their retirement plans? A couple of economists examined six years of data for about 35,000 households, and discovered that men built riskier stock portfolios than women. (The stock market didn't reward their high risk tolerance; men's returns were 0.93 percent *lower* than women's,[7] just so you know.)

As a financial advisor I used to see this all the time, across all age groups: women were afraid to pick the wrong investments, even though the most seasoned fund managers fail at it *consistently*.[8] (They still get paid big bucks in an industry where the entry-level salary for an analyst at a mid-performing hedge fund is $335,000,[9] with the operative word here being "mid-performing").

When it comes to difficult conversations, failure is perceived as when the other person doesn't change. You may fear that he does not respect you enough to change or does not care enough for some reason.

You have read, and will read, that we cannot truly change someone else. That is also something you inherently know.

> *You may fail in terms of things not turning out as you'd like. But, you did not fail. Failure is not attempting the conversation.*

You are successful because you did it! You had the courage to face the fear and do it anyway! That is success that comes with a high reward.

Fear of Hurting Someone Else

As women, we don't like to be hurt and we especially don't like to hurt others. Here is an example of that from my daughter Dani and her high school debate teammate. They participate in tournaments against other schools almost every weekend. Last Saturday she and her partner, let's call him Decimus, felt like they were rocking. Out of the five rounds, they knew that they had won four, so even when they didn't know yet how they'd done in the fifth round, they were feeling confident they'd place in the finals.

At the end of the day there was a ceremony to celebrate the winners, and everyone attended. As the judges announced each place, my daughter's team grew more and more nervous. Finally, the winners were announced and it wasn't them!

Disappointed, they went to ask their coach how they had done in the fifth round. To their surprise the coach told them they had won. Then he said, "Wait a minute. You won every time!" And that's when they realized the judge had given the first prize trophy—publicly—to another team!

When Dani and Decimus understood the mistake they were happy, but at the same time Dani felt sorry for the other team. She knew they had to have a difficult conversation with them, and she was worried about hurting their feelings.

Immediately, my daughter told her partner, "We have to be *very* cautious and plan how we will tell them because we don't want to hurt their fee . . ." She hadn't finished her sentence when her partner, Decimus, yelled from one side to the cafeteria to the other, "FERGUS! Give me MY trophy!"

When my daughter told me this story, I immediately knew I had to share it with you. I knew men and women would smile and say, "Yep. That's how it is. Men tend to handle things straight on and other men usually respond well to it."

> *While it's good to be considerate, if you take it too far you may be underestimating the other person's capacity to deal with difficulties.*

You may be treating a guy as if he were nothing more than a hairy woman if you think you'll hurt his feelings easily.

Look at how Gail Evans explains it in her book *Play like a Man Win like a Woman: What Men Know About Success That Women Need to Learn:*

Men like to fight. They start fighting with each other when they're young, and they keep fighting until there's no fight left in them . . . I know a nursing home attendant who says she has to break up fistfights between two octogenarians over rocking space on the front porch.

Can you imagine those grandpas fighting? Adorable! But wait, I haven't told you my favorite part of her arguments:

To a man, a fight is part of the game. One of you wins, one of you loses, and then the winner buys the loser a drink.

You have to leave your opponent breathing, so you can play again.

Don't tell me you didn't know this to be true! Ms. Evans advice? "He's a lot more likely to enjoy the process than you are, which is all the more reason for you to get it over with quickly."[10]

There you have it. Still, that's a generalization, not an absolute, and in some of your "combats" you will have a female "opponent." This means you may hurt someone's feelings when you are straightforward. It is a risk. However, when handled effectively, this is diminished. Someone may be overly sensitive and you can't control that. You need to continue on just as before the conversation happened. You need to get back to normal ASAP.

The bottom line is that you can't let this worry stop you from facing someone. If you do, you have allowed the other person to manipulate you (whether or not they are aware of it) into accepting the behavior. Just because she might get her feelings hurt does not mean you shouldn't have the conversation.

Fear of Getting What You Want

Doesn't it seem a bit absurd to be afraid to get your way? You want something and then you are afraid of getting it? However, when you think about it, this fear makes sense. Maybe you find it difficult to ask for a promotion. You know you want it but if you get it, what will come with it? Perhaps your peers will not like you or you won't know how to deal with friends you will be supervising.

Whatever the issue is for you, only you can weigh the risk versus the reward. Just make sure fear isn't stopping you! Linda Tarr-Whelan recounts what former secretary-general of the United Nations Koki Annan, whom she describes as "a very wise man and promoter of women's equality" replied when asked why there weren't more women in top civil service UN jobs:

> I've always been interested in seeing talented colleagues move up . . . So, whenever an opening for a promotion was advertised, I often said to a talented person, "You should apply for this job." Women almost universally told me they weren't experienced enough or didn't have sufficient background. I never had a man say anything but "Thank you, I will apply."[11]

Actually, this is an area where others can learn from African American women: 22 percent of black professional women aspire to a powerful position with a prestigious title, compared with just eight percent of white professional women.[12]

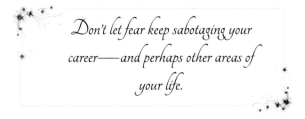

Don't let fear keep sabotaging your career—and perhaps other areas of your life.

At one of my workshops, Judith, an attendee, told me her story. Her firm posted a position that she had been wanting for quite a while. When she saw it, she was nervous about applying and really doubted her abilities. If she was promoted, she would have to train new employees and she saw her training abilities as a weakness. Despite her reservations, she applied.

She confessed to me that on more than one occasion she almost took her name out of the running. Her negative self-fears would creep in and she'd hear herself think things like, "I can't do this." "They wouldn't promote me." "I'm not good enough."

"I'm not smart enough." If you've compared yourself only with people you think are better than you, or you've focused on what you don't have rather than on what you have (and who hasn't?), you've experienced what Judith was going through. But she didn't listen to her own negative voice and instead decided to think positively.

To her surprise, she got the job! The change was scary at first, but well worth it. Fast-forward and she couldn't imagine anything better. She was amazed at how much she loves training new employees and the job in general. She has no regrets.

This is a lesson for me, for sure! Don't let fear stop you. Many women in my travels have shared how they let fear stop them from getting what they want. Remember, be like Judith and you might just get what you want too.

Fear of Intimacy

Now aren't we just being crazy? Nope. In fact, the fear of intimacy used to be a big one for me but I didn't realize it. I made choices in my dating life based on which man did not want intimacy. I'm talking about the kind of intimacy where you are close and can talk to each other about hopes, fears, and dreams. Where you feel like you can tell this person almost anything (or absolutely anything). I was afraid of anyone trying to be that close to me. I wasn't used to it and it was not comfortable.

Due to my discomfort with intimacy, I chose the wrong man to marry. This affected many years of my life and would probably have affected the rest of it had I not decided to change. I did not have many difficult conversations with him simply because that was too intimate. However, I've worked through it and you can too. Not that I'm there yet, but I'm certainly progressing and I'm not going to let the fear of intimacy stop me from stating what I want or need. Don't let it stop you either.

Fear of Not Being Liked

Have you heard the famous quote by Deepak Chopra, "What other people think of you is none of your business"? What if someone doesn't like you? Do you really care so much about what she thinks? Sometimes you need to care, but typically we as women are far too afraid that someone won't like us.

As I told you in the introduction, I went through a long period of my life where I cared so much about what other people thought of me that it controlled many of my actions. Until one day I started taking a hard look at myself and decided to change. I mentioned that the catalyst had been my sister, but I also want to share with you that I changed how I thought. I make it sound simple but I just began by thinking each time I wanted someone to like me, "Do I really care what that person thinks of me?" Most of the time it was no, no I don't.

We need to care enough but not so much that others rule our lives.

Please shower. Please wear deodorant. Care, at least some, what others think! But, as women, we tend to take it too far.

If you are anything like I was, trust me, you can change. It just takes effort and practice. But first, just become aware when you are caring more than you should and letting others control your life. Perhaps keep a journal or make notes on your phone when you care too much what others think. The first step is becoming aware and then you can change.

You know, I'm pretty outgoing and friendly and some people won't like that. I'm also hilarious, in my own mind, but some people won't like that. I'm the kind of person who speaks to strangers and strikes up conversations and some people won't like that. I'm an embarrassment sometimes so not everyone likes me. And, guess what? That's okay!

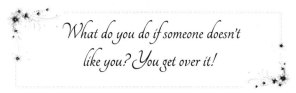

What do you do if someone doesn't like you? You get over it!

But, hey, I like you and if you like me, then we have a mutual admiration society and that's fine by me.

Fear of Being Considered a "Witch"

We have framed it politely here but we all know what we mean by "witch." Women recognize that we'll receive that label if we are thought of as aggressive. Picture this:

> *The boss is trying to fill an important position. In the interview a male applicant boasts about his abilities, explains why he's the best person for the job, and urges the boss to pick him. After the man leaves, the boss compliments by calling him aggressive . . . A woman [shows similar behaviors, and] the boss finds her domineering, overbearing, difficult. After she leaves the boss criticizes her by calling her aggressive.*[13]

Sound familiar?

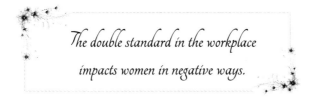

The double standard in the workplace

impacts women in negative ways.

I remember distinctly when a man I had known a long time was yelling at me, "You're a 'witch'!" over and over because I had the courage to finally speak my mind. This person had never reacted to me like that but at that moment I understood *I had taken away his power*. He strongly objected that I stood up for myself now. I was no longer going to get walked on and I had become more powerful. No longer would I be abused.

Acknowledge the fear. Don't blame yourself for feeling it. It's real. Acknowledge it and control it. Remember that learning to conduct difficult conversations without being aggressive and without being a doormat is a skill that can be developed.

Techniques for Calming Your Fears

Tell Yourself, "STOP IT!"

There is no benefit at all in worrying. Even if you are absolutely sure (and correct) this conversation will not turn out the way you want, you have gained nothing by worrying!

What's the cure then? Here's what works for me. When I start to worry about a conversation, I tell myself (yes, sometimes out loud), "Stop it." Then I push the worry out of my head. Then it creeps back in and I do the same thing. "Stop it!"

Depending on the depth of the worry, I sometimes have to tell myself this over and over again. The next step is not to let the negative thoughts keep me from attaining my goals or at least trying. Despite the negative fears, I keep going.

If you'd like to see a funny video on this, look up *Bob Newhart Stop It* (it's really funny!) I saw it recently, and it perfectly represents what I use!

This *Stop It* technique is similar to one that Dr. Catherine Pittman, a licensed clinical psychologist in private practice in South Bend, Indiana, recommends. Dr. Pittman prescribes using the *thought stopping* technique I just told you I use *and then* replacing the thought with another thought—anything, as long as it's captivating and preferably pleasant.

"By replacing the anxiety provoking thought with something else that engages your mind," she says, "you make it more likely that you won't return to that thought."

You can have something that is your go-to positive thought. Here are some ideas: I have great friends. My family loves me. I love chocolate cake. Whatever you like! The chocolate cake one makes me want some though so maybe that one isn't so good.

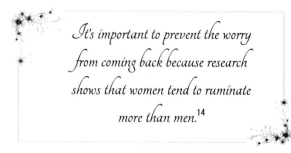

It's important to prevent the worry from coming back because research shows that women tend to ruminate more than men.[14]

The more you ruminate, the less likely you are to get things accomplished. You may get in your own way of active problem solving, so unless you stop your overthinking you may make yourself not only more stressed, but less effective. Stop it!

And speaking of ruminating, did you know that women are also more likely than men to focus on negative aspects of themselves, and this may be one more reason why you worry? I'm going to say that yes—you did know that.

> *We tend to be overly critical of ourselves in ways that men are usually not of themselves.*[15]

Let me guess, you don't love your hair, skin, height or weight? And, those are just the physical things. You are also critical of the aspects of how you do your job.

When I read *The Confidence Code* by Katty Kay and Claire Shipman, I was stunned to find out that even powerful women such as WNBA (Women's National Basketball Association) stars have trouble in this area. They ruminate over their abilities and their mistakes just like all of us. Despite her prowess on the court, one of the athletes, Crystal Langhorne, said that she struggles with confidence.

She stated that male (NBA) players seem to shrug off a bad game more easily, whereas she tends to ruminate over a loss. She also admitted that at times her lack of confidence has to do with her people pleasing side and her desire to play well for everyone around her. You have read how pleasing others was my issue too, and how that lead to a lot of worry.

Schedule Your Worry

Another technique I use to stop worrying is to actually schedule the worry. "I'll worry about it tomorrow," or "I'll worry about it in ten minutes." It takes practice, but it works. This works whether you are going to have a difficult conversation or just handle something else perceived as difficult.

One time about 15 years ago I was asked to speak for a group of miners in Tennessee. I was so nervous because the management had requested that a man come and speak to them and NOT a woman and since I was not a man, how could they possibly see me as qualified? At least that was my interpretation at the time.

As soon as I was invited I scheduled my worry. When a thought crept in my head about how I was nervous, I'd simply say, "I'm not going to worry about that for two weeks." And then, "I'm not going to worry about that for one week." And so on and so on until the morning of my presentation. I said, "I am not going to ruin this last ten minutes. I can worry right before I speak." Sometimes I had to repeat the line over and over but it worked.

I did end up worrying, but only for small spurts, and never had the full worry time I had scheduled. It was so effective, that I began using it for all kinds of small and large things I worried about daily.

And, I am happy to report the miners loved the presentation. It was such a fun experience and I'll always remember how I won over those tough men despite my worry.

Here's another idea, courtesy of Dr. Hazlett-Stevens, assistant professor of psychology at the University of Nevada in Reno, Nevada: suppose the worst did happen.[16] I have done something similar; I've asked myself, "Who's gonna die if this doesn't turn out as I'd like?" And since the answer is usually *no one*, having asked that question allows me to bring things back into perspective.

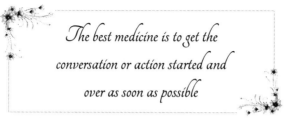

The best medicine is to get the conversation or action started and over as soon as possible

We have already discussed how putting off a difficult conversation is not helpful. But c'mon, you knew that!

Commit to 20 Seconds of Courage

Last week my daughter and I were watching *We Bought a Zoo* with my boyfriend Matt Damon (I wish this meant he was sitting next to me!) Have you watched it? We loved it. I love any movie that allows me to collect one of those mother-and-daughter-crying-together-watching-a-chick-flick memories.

Throughout the movie Matt repeats the phrase "20 seconds of courage." He tells his kids several stories of times when he was afraid of taking a risk, and he made himself do what he had to do by telling himself, "All you need is 20 seconds, no more than that. Only 20 seconds. You can do it *because* it's only 20 seconds."

In the movie Matt is a widower who wants to buy a zoo to provide a healthier and happier life to his son and to his *adorable* daughter, but he's worried about whether he'll be able to keep it going—it's a huge responsibility! So he gets 20 seconds of courage and buys it. Later in the movie he tells his kids the story of how he was once walking down a street when, through a glass window, he saw the most beautiful woman in the world sitting at a restaurant table. He counted for 20 seconds and that gave him enough time to walk into the café (five seconds) and talk to her (15 seconds). That woman was their mom. Tissue, anyone?

Oh, now don't go buy your own zoo and blame me for it, though.

Anyway, after we watched the movie my daughter and I started getting ready for bed. I'm in my room when I hear her yell "MOM!" from the bathroom. What happened? I wondered, and I ran to find out. "A spider!" she yelled. "A big one!" she added. She usually catches insects with a piece of cardboard and an empty jar (that we keep just for this purpose) so we can throw them out of the house. But this time she was scared of the big spider. "Only 20 seconds," I said. And that's all it took.

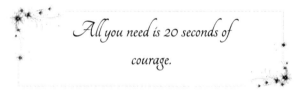

All you need is 20 seconds of courage.

She caught it! It did end up being a piece of lint (pause for effect) from my new bathrobe and not a spider, but still, she faced her fear for 20 seconds!

If you can get yourself to do something for 20 seconds, the worst part will probably be over.

Not long ago I was at a conference surrounded by a group of successful motivational speakers and life coaches. We were exchanging tricks, so to speak. I asked them, "What do you tell someone who has to do something she doesn't want to do, such as cold-calling prospective clients?" I was hoping to get some type of miraculous recipe I didn't know about, considering the group I asked. Want to know what they said? "Just make the first call." Isn't that the 20 seconds prescription?

Someone else added a great suggestion. She said, "Since most people don't like to cold-call because they don't want to hear "No," just reward yourself whenever you get a "No." That is a fantastic idea, isn't it? I mean, we already know the behavior that gets rewarded gets repeated, so why not use it to help us do what we dread?

There you have it. The magic recipe to get the guts you need to go face that difficult conversation: whenever you need to face a challenge in life, or an unpleasant task, just think of Matt Damon and his 20 seconds. I know it puts a smile on my face.

Practice to Make It Permanent

Even if you handle a difficult conversation the perfect way, sometimes your fears will come true. People may still consider you to be too aggressive or they may reject you, etc. But isn't that okay?

> *If we go around not saying things just because of fear then we have no one to blame but ourselves when things don't change.*

Rejection was a big fear of mine, which was one reason I used to avoid difficult conversations. One day I realized rejection wasn't as bad as the amount of stress I had fearing the rejection. The things that bothered me kept bothering me and didn't naturally go away like I had hoped. Being rejected was better than the powerlessness and stress I was feeling. So I changed.

I make it sound easy, but it wasn't. I had programmed myself to avoid rather than confront for so long that it took a lot to
muster up the courage each time. It's not that I don't have a bit
of fear now but I can act despite the fear and am always glad I
did.

The process of change takes three steps: awareness of the
problem (including your role), a strategy to change (which this
book is giving you), and discipline to follow through.

Some people say the longer you've had a habit, the harder it
is to break. David J. Lieberman, Ph.D., author of *Instant Analysis: How to Understand and Change the 100 Most Common,
Annoying, Puzzling, Self-Defeating Behaviors and Habits* says
it's not the time associated with the habit per se, but the lack of
awareness. He explains that "the longer you engage in a behavior, the more unaware you become of the actual activity." Dr.
Lieberman says habits are dead processes we do over and over
without thinking, and that's why bringing attention to a habit
breathes life into it so it's no longer mechanical. And that's how
we can stop it.[17]

After I became aware, the strategy I used was to think about
how it felt when I didn't stand up for what I wanted. I would
think about the powerlessness I felt and how things didn't
change naturally.

Each time I needed to talk to someone about something I
perceived as difficult, I would remind myself of the consequences of not doing it. This reminder gave me the discipline.
Discipline is not something we're born with—it's something we
cultivate.

You have probably heard some people claim that it takes 21
days to change a habit. Allow me to adjust that a bit. It might just
take 30 seconds. That's because your motivation is a big part of

how quickly a habit will change. Let's say you go to the doctor and she says that if you stop smoking today you will live another 40 years, but if you don't, you will die tomorrow. Let's assume you believe the doctor. Will you quit smoking today? Yes, you will! It's because you have the motivation to quit. The strategy is not much of a strategy except to quit right now and the discipline is easier since death is not a great option.

Next time you want to change a habit, start by giving yourself a reason to quit that's stronger than the habit.

Most of the time, however, you will need longer: 21 days *or more* (yes, *or more*. The 21 days is a myth.)[19] The point is when you are truly motivated to change, it won't take you as long as when you are not motivated. If change were easy, there would be no need for nicotine patches or weight loss groups.

You have the habit of avoiding difficult conversations, so break it. (Again, that sounds so easy!) Think about a conversation you have avoided. Did your avoidance make it better? Were you glad you didn't say anything? What could have been different if you had spoken up? How would you have felt if you had spoken up? If you answer these questions and realize that you can have a better life if you speak up, then you may not need the full 21 days to break the avoidance habit.

Have the courage but also go easy on yourself. There will be times when you will still avoid but then ask yourself the questions in the paragraph above and really think about it. Then, you may still get the courage or you may be able to use it the next time. Practice doesn't make perfect—perfection doesn't exist. But practice turns any behavior into a habit and makes it *permanent*, which helps reduce fear and worry! Begin today by having that conversation you have been avoiding.

What Did You Learn?

Take some time to process what you read. Write a few notes. What did you learn in this chapter that you will use in your next difficult conversation? Do you even read this *What Did You Learn* section? I am fearful that you won't. But, hey, I'm working on controlling my fears so BAM! I just let that fear go. Now it's time for you to let go of those fears and worries. You can do it, you are a WikiWoman. Oh, don't know what that means? Go to page five and then come back and check the fears you will work on conquering:

- ☐ Fear of harm
- ☐ Fear of rejection
- ☐ Fear of loss of a relationship
- ☐ Fear of anger
- ☐ Fear of saying the wrong thing
- ☐ Fear of being seen as selfish
- ☐ Fear of failing
- ☐ Fear of hurting someone else
- ☐ Fear of getting what you want
- ☐ Fear of intimacy
- ☐ Fear of not being liked
- ☐ Fear of being considered too aggressive (or a "witch")

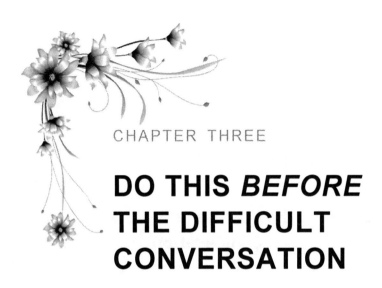

CHAPTER THREE

DO THIS *BEFORE* THE DIFFICULT CONVERSATION

*A*braham Lincoln said, "If I had eight hours to chop down a tree, I'd spend six hours sharpening my axe." The good news is you will likely spend a lot less than six hours. Let's get started!

The time you invest in preparing will be time well spent, believe me—if nothing else, you'll feel more confident. I have compiled a list of things to do before the difficult conversation to help you prepare. This list isn't as daunting as it seems. I've numbered the items to help you memorize them (if you want to), but you can work on them in any order.

1. Assess the **cost** against the benefit of having the difficult conversation.
2. Have a clear and realistic **objective**.
3. Determine your **reserve** value.

4. Assume **positive** intent and outcome.
5. Prepare your **plan B.**
6. Plan your **environment.**
7. Prepare your **exit line.**
8. Decide on your **stance.**
9. Raise your **confidence.**
10. Prepare your **script** using the NO FEAR™ method.

1. Assess the Cost-Benefit of Having the Conversation

I always encourage women to become more assertive and stand up for themselves. However, in life there are times when it's really not worth it to try to get people to change their behavior.

To pick your battle, ask yourself the following questions:

- Is approaching the offender dangerous?

- Is the change I want even possible?

- Am I sweating the small stuff or being a perfectionist?

- Is this even my battle?

- Would I be better yielding as an act of love?

We need to pick our battles.

Your Safety Comes First

When dealing with people that can harm you, you need to get professional help before attempting to address the situation. If you suspect that the person you're considering confronting suffers from a psychological disorder (such as narcissism, sadism, sociopathic personality, etc.) be even more aware than ever that your safety is top priority at all times. Misogynists, for instance, are men who despise, dislike, or have strong prejudices against women, and they experience confrontations, challenges, or complaints about their behavior as assaults on them, and respond accordingly.[1]

> *You don't need to be a psychologist. Just follow your gut feelings, and if something doesn't feel right, avoid it.*

As a manager, I once had to take part in firing an employee who was known for being aggressive, so we prepared. After we fired him, despite what we knew of him, we were surprised that he stormed out tearing things down as he left. The most surprising thing is that he threatened to kill me. Yes, me. Not any other manager, but me. I'm not sure why (because I was the prettiest? Nah—more likely because I was the only female manager) but it was scary. The funny thing is that later on another restaurant where he was applying called and asked me for a reference!

In this case of the crazy employee, we had to have the conversation. Although we thought we had prepared, I don't know what we would have done if he had actually lunged at me. The bottom line is, be careful and expect the unexpected when dealing with unstable people.

Some Changes Are Not Possible

Are you surprised to hear that someone like me (who thrives to empower and motivate women to reach their full potential) uses the word impossible? Yes, I do.

Let me explain. It took me a long time to accept the hard truth that there are things in life that are beyond my control, no matter how hard I try or how smart I am (or think I am.) That is because my mom, a self-made woman who was always a role model of strength and tenacity, always told me that "everything was possible," and that "I could do anything I set my mind to." (Well, come to think about it, she also told me that it was Santa Claus who had given me my first bike.)

Do you still believe people can change anything, and if they don't it is just because they don't want to or don't work hard enough at it? It would be nice if that were true, but it's not. My best advice is to remind yourself of *The Serenity Prayer*:

> *God, grant me the serenity to accept the things I cannot change, the courage to change the things I can, and the wisdom to know the difference.*

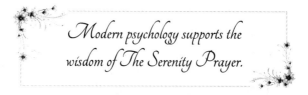

Modern psychology supports the wisdom of The Serenity Prayer.

There are some things about ourselves that can be changed, others that cannot, and still some others that can be changed only with extreme difficulty.[2]

Are You Being Too Thin-Skinned?

Do you need thicker skin? I don't mean to discount your feelings. What the other person did or said may be a big deal to you, but before you act on your feelings, it's worth taking some time to ask yourself if you're perceiving the offense in its correct proportion. You may even need an unbiased opinion from a neutral third party.

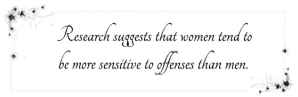

Research suggests that women tend to be more sensitive to offenses than men.

For instance, women report more intense anger to transgressions, their anger takes longer to dissipate, they take longer to reconcile, and they show increased heart rate following recall of a conflict and role-playing a reaction to it.[3] This doesn't mean that you personally are more sensitive, but it may make it worth it to explore your options.

Two researchers from the University of Waterloo wanted to explore why women apologize more than men.[4] So they recruited a group of men and a group of women and asked them to keep a daily diary where, every night, they'd record the offenses they had committed or received, and whether an apology had been deserved and or had been offered. They also recorded the circumstances around that event.

What the study ended up finding may surprise you. The reason women apologize more is because they perceive they offend more. And the reason men apologize less is because they have a higher threshold for what constitutes offensive behavior. If there's no offense then there's no reason to apologize, right? So they don't.

In my workshops for women they all crack up when I share the explanation I once read about why men don't ask for directions. It's because they don't know they're lost. And it's not a joke! If they may be a bit lost about their location, it's not hard to believe they may be lost that they offended us.

How can you apply these findings to your life? Well, how about considering that sometimes others may not be aware their behavior is offending you before assuming they don't care.

Is it even your battle?

Sure, sometimes you need to get into another person's battles. I remember hearing stories about women being attacked and strangers just watching and not helping. Those stories are so sad and you might decide it is worth it to get into, especially by calling the police.

In most cases, you won't have such a drastic decision. Usually, you need to mind your bees wax (as we used to say in grade school) and stay out of it. How do you know? Ask yourself, how does this impact me? And, if your only answer is that your friend is upset, you probably need to stay out of it.

As a person who has been deeply hurt by another, I have had a lot of friends stick by me but they never attacked him. They did support me but didn't fight my actual battle. I had to do that.

Yielding as an Act of Love

I don't remember how many times I had this conversation with my 80 something mother:

Me: "Mom? Did you move the papers I left here?"

Mom: "Of course not. I *never* touch your papers."

Me: "Well, I know I left them here before leaving for Atlanta, and you're the only one who has been in the house since, so . . ."

Mom: "I told you. I *never* touch your papers. I would remember if I had. You have a bad memory, so you move them and then you forget you did. "

Me: "I don't have bad memory mom. And you *do* move my papers. Remember when . . .?"

Until one day I thought, is it really worth it asking her? Making her feel uncomfortable? Straining our relationship a bit? And the answers were no, no, and no. Ever since, when I ask her about my papers and she says she never touches them I just say "Okay, thank you."

Now you may be wondering why do I even ask her. I've wondered that myself. I guess I do have a bad memory.

Be Honest with Yourself

If you decide not to go through with the difficult conversation, the challenge will be for you to be honest with yourself and detached enough to decide if you're talking yourself out of having the conversation because of realistic reasons, or just because you're rationalizing your fears.

Think of a conversation you wanted to have but you didn't. Did you talk yourself out of it? As we move further, think about it and decide how you could have handled it. This will prepare you for the next time.

2. Have a Clear and Realistic Objective

How many times have you gone into a difficult conversation without having first paused, reflected, and determined what your objective was?

Your answer here: _____.

You don't remember? I don't either. But I know I have. The older I get, the less impulsive I am, but I am a fast person, so in the past I tended to react to aggressions pretty quickly, acting mostly on emotion, and without having asked myself, what do I want to get out of this encounter?

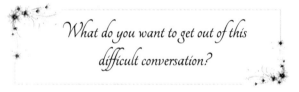

What do you want to get out of this difficult conversation?

You can have more than one objective, and unless you are clear beforehand in your priorities, your approach may reflect indecisiveness or uncertainty. And those are interpreted as weaknesses.

On those occasions when you have conflicting objectives, it is fundamental that you fight your internal battle in private, before facing the other party.

Unless your priorities are crystal clear you may end up sweating the small stuff or becoming a doormat. Lack of a clear objective and priorities may also have other negative consequences. And once you've had your difficult conversation, it will be too late to take it back.

As an example, let me share a story that my sister Rocio told me. Rocio means dew in Spanish, but you don't need to worry about pronouncing it—her nickname is Rosca, which translates to doughnut, so we'll just call her Doughnut. Her daughter Ofelia is a freshman at a university in Bogota, Colombia, where she's studying fashion design.

A few months ago, Ofelia started coming home, and instead of chatting with the family about her day, she would go to her room and close the door. Knowing that her daughter is an introvert, my sister Doughnut left her alone, until her other daughter told her mom that Ofelia was crying almost every day, but didn't want their mom to know.

That's when my sister started to put two and two together: her grades had been sliding and she didn't seem to enjoy college as much. Being a fashion designer had been her dream since she was a small child, and now she seemed to dread going to school. So my sister, worried, decided to confront her and find out what was happening.

Ofelia opened up to her mother. She told her that her sewing teacher didn't like her. She shared that the teacher said, "You should not be here. You don't see well, and you're never going to be good at this." She broke down in tears. Ofelia has strabismus, which is a disorder of vision that prevents her from having both her eyes directed at the same object at the same time, so it is true that she struggles in the sewing class. Strabismus is operable, but her mother assumed that she needed to wait until Ofelia was older to get the surgery.

Long story short, this teacher was making Ofelia's life miserable. When she asked a question, the teacher would say, "I already explained that. You were not paying attention and I won't explain it again just for you."

No wonder she dreaded going to school. "I was ready to give the teacher a piece of my mind. I was furious," Doughnut later told me, and I could completely understand. I bet you do too.

"I wish I could tell you that I didn't call the teacher because I am so good at emotional control," my sister told me, and added, "But I won't because it wouldn't be true. I would have called the teacher right then if I had her number." And that would have been a mistake. A big mistake.

At that point, she hadn't had the time to consider her possible objectives when talking to the teacher. These objectives could have been one or more of the following:

- to help the teacher understand how putting limits on Ofelia could psychologically affect her,

- to educate the teacher on the advantages of positive motivation rather than criticism,

- to gently warn the teacher that if her behavior persisted she would make a big deal with the principal,

- to make the teacher cry as she had made Ofelia cry,

- or simply to ask her to stop her bullying behavior.

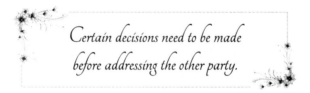

Certain decisions need to be made before addressing the other party.

My sister's tone, stance, word selection, and even the duration of the conversation would need to be different depending on her objective. And having an objective would help her stay focused.

Doughnut decided it was best if Ofelia handled the situation. They had a long conversation about the importance of standing up for yourself, and they came to a couple agreements:

- First, Ofelia would breathe deeply before going to class, try to be calm and open-minded, and she would listen to this teacher assuming good intent.

- Their second agreement was that if the teacher started putting her down her Ofelia was going to say, "I believe I can be as good as anybody else at this, and I would appreciate it if you respected that." And if the criticism persisted, she would just stand up and go to the dean's office.

Doughnut added, "At that point I was really happy that I hadn't called the teacher the day before, when I was burning hot. If I had called right then and there, in front of my child, in order to release my frustration, I would have harmed my kid. It would have caused her anxiety. I would have been a bad role model of emotional control. And the worst part would have been that my daughter would have never trusted me again. And when in the future another bully (maybe a more dangerous one) harassed her, she wouldn't have been comfortable coming to me."

Do you see how important it is to consciously and rationally set an objective, stick to it (unless an extreme change in conditions occurs), and plan your strategy in a manner that supports that objective?

I'm happy to report that now this teacher treats my niece with respect. Ofelia is no longer afraid of going to school. Oh, and a month later, she had eye surgery and the problem has been corrected!

3. Determine Your Reserve Value

Imagine that you want to sell the castle where you live. It used to be worth millions but you're thinking it has depreciated so you'll list it for $100K. Don't faint, this is just an example.

Isn't it true that even before listing you have already decided what the minimum offer you'd sell it for is? In this case, let's say that you list it at $100K but if someone offers you $90K you'll close the deal. In that case the $90K is your reserve value.

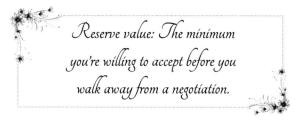

Reserve value: The minimum you're willing to accept before you walk away from a negotiation.

Most people have a reserve value for their real estate, but not for other negotiations.

It doesn't have to be a monetary value. Having a reserve value before "sitting at the negotiation table" saves you from having to assess an offer on the fly and in the heat of the conversation. That's the whole idea of preparation.

Another benefit of determining your reserve value is that it kind of forces you to make your objective measurable and less subjective. Here's an example: if your goal is to have your partner help you with the dishes after dinner, that's kind of vague. But, when you think that the minimum you will agree on is that the other person places the dirty dishes into the dishwasher every other day, now that's more specific.

4. Assume Positive Intent and Outcome

Positive Intent

It is simply easier sometimes to just jump to a negative assumption of other people's motives and actions. In fact, we often don't think of any other option.

Here's an example: I get my energy from other people and when I'm teaching I'm excited and it flows from me. When I first began teaching workshops, you could multiply my excitement by 100 because I was so happy to be doing my dream job. After the workshop, I would look at the evaluations and every single time at least one person would write "She's too happy. It's fake." They assumed I was acting happy when I was actually really happy. There were times I wanted to run out of the room and yell, "I really am happy!" but I refrained.

A positive mindset is even more important in difficult conversations. Instead of thinking, "He just doesn't like me," or "She's just trying to be difficult," or even "There is no way that Belinda is going to listen," think something positive. Perhaps you are misreading the other person. If your first thought is negative, take a moment and just think about how you could turn it to something positive.

> *Being positive is not being naïve. It is just giving the benefit of the doubt and giving yourself the chance to trust and keep a positive attitude toward life.*

One phrase that helps me is, "Don't think for a minute that you're an expert at mind reading." I love that because too often I've tried to mind read by jumping to conclusions. Use that and it will help you navigate difficult conversations more smoothly, but it will also have other benefits.

Since the 1960s an increasing body of research has demonstrated a consistent tendency of healthy, successful people to think in generally positive ways.[5] So be healthier and more successful and think positively!

Positive Outcome: Everyone Wins

One of the main enemies of successful conflict resolution is our assumption that for one side to win, the other has to lose.

Yes, behaving like a doormat is a lose-win proposition (you lose, they win), and being demanding and manipulative is a win-lose proposition (you win, they lose), but you must remember there is an everyone-wins strategy. It's called collaboration or problem-solving.

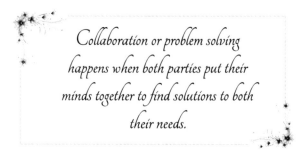

Collaboration or problem solving happens when both parties put their minds together to find solutions to both their needs.

Nobody has to lose. Assume that, and you'll come to the negotiation table with the right attitude.

5. Prepare Your Plan B

At the time I started writing this book, my daughter was applying to college, and she had plans A, B, C, and D.

- Plan A was Georgetown, which is the university she really wanted to attend.

- In case they didn't accept her, she had plan B, which included Yale, Duke, and Penn. Since all of them are highly selective she thought she needed a plan C.

- Plan C was the University of Oklahoma, because they'd offer her free tuition if she won a competition to become a National Merit Scholar.

- And plan D? Plan D was in case no highly selective college admitted her and she didn't win the competition. Plan D included two universities whose names I couldn't pronounce. Seriously.

In contrast, I've heard of many people who apply to *only one* college, without a plan B. Have you heard any stories of someone getting a rejection letter, panicking (along with his or her parents), jumping into the family car, driving from one state to another to apply in person to another college on the last day of the deadline? I have.

That seems like a lot of unnecessary stress.

Think for a minute about companies that have gone belly up: Circuit City, Blockbuster, and Polaroid, for instance. They stuck to their business model and didn't seem to have a plan B, so when circumstances turned out not to be as they predicted, their model didn't work, and they perished.

What about my daughter? Once she got her acceptance letters, she ended up narrowing her choice to Boudoin (which by now I knew how to pronounce), Duke, and Georgetown. We visited all of them, and she confirmed that it was Georgetown that made her heart sing.

If nothing else, having had backup plans allowed her to feel even more confident that her plan A was the best.

But let's go back to *you* having a plan B before facing that difficult conversation.

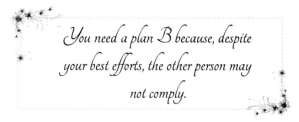

You need a plan B because, despite your best efforts, the other person may not comply.

Yogi Berra once said, "If the people don't want to come out to the ballpark, nobody's going to stop them." That's why it's important to ponder what your options will be if the person you're having a difficult conversation with refuses to cooperate. Will you insist? Will you escalate it to your supervisor? Will you let it go?

A few years ago a woman, let's call her Lilibeth, attended one of my workshops on assertive communication just for women. During the break she approached me for advice. She looked extremely anxious and sad. I asked, "What's going on Lilibeth?"

She said, looking down, "My boss tells me *constantly* that I remind him of his ex-wife. And I know he doesn't like her." Ouch.

Wait. It gets worse. Lilibeth went on to tell me that the week before, at an office lunch party, he walked next to her, looked at the chicken plate she had ordered, and commented, "What a nice pair of breasts you have there." The poor woman was psychologically drained and felt completely powerless. "Do you think that man is someone open to having a difficult conversation?" I asked Lilibeth.

She said, "This has been going on for a long time!" (Notice that she didn't answer my question.)

We talked about how she had approached him in the past, and what she could do better this time. I am an optimist, but in this case I didn't really think this man respected her enough to listen to what she had to say, so I moved fast and considered alternatives (a.k.a. potential plan B's).

"Is there an HR department at your company?" I asked.

"No," she said, "we're a small firm."

"Okay then. Who is your supervisor's boss?"

"He's the owner."

My obvious next question was, "What is so amazing about this job that has kept you there in spite of the damage this man is doing to your self-esteem and to your mental health?"

"Well," she said, "I've been here for 12 years."

Oh, my goodness. Imagine getting that kind of mental junk in your head periodically over 12 years! No wonder she had no strength to find another job, or had been so devalued that she didn't think she'd find anything! I've been in an abusive marriage, and believe me, some abusers would need to stick with professional help for a long, long time, before others could see a change. And there are no guarantees.

I'll give you some ideas in the following chapters, but my point here is that you need to take time to think about how to handle these types of situations. Had I been Lilibeth, I would have started an active job search *before* going into the difficult conversation, so if this man dismissed my request I'd have a plan B ready to go.

6. Plan Your Environment

Pema Chodron, who has been referred to as "a Buddhist nun for regular folks" narrates how she participated in sweat lodges when she was young. A sweat lodge is a hut, typically dome-shaped and made with natural materials, used by North American Indians for ritual steam baths as a means of purification.

Chodron says, "I would always sit by the flap covering the entrance to the sweat lodge. That way, if things got too intense, I could quickly, easily duck out."[6]

That's exactly what we mean by controlling your environment. But there's more.

Plan When and Where

It is important to plan when and where to have the conversation. For instance, do you know when the best time to ask for a raise is? I recommend after lunch or very early in the morning, before work starts. And what are the best days? Tuesdays, Wednesdays, or Thursdays.

Controlling when and where to have that conversation may make a difference in the outcome. You need to ask yourself questions such as, should we meet at her place, my place, or a neutral place?

I prefer to meet at the other person's place, so she feels more relaxed and comfortable and at the same time I can leave when

I want. Wherever you choose, keep in mind that a friendly environment invites dialogue, and a place where you can sit closely (perhaps without a desk creating a barrier between you) may create the idea you're a team working together on solving a problem. What is your preference for this particular conversation? It may depend on your personality.

Set an Appointment or Stop by?

I have found that it tends to go more smoothly if you just stop by without preparing the person first. Of course this depends on the circumstances, but if you pop in unannounced, the person doesn't have time to get nervous or worry about what you might say and therefore make the conversation more difficult.

Other Details

There are other details you may want to consider. And again, how much time you devote to planning your strategy will need to be commensurate to the importance of each case. In some instances, it won't matter, and in others the time is crucial. Of course, you don't want to over prepare or waste so much time thinking that you end up becoming a worrier.

Here's an example. I once met a girl who was very sensitive. She decided to confront her supervisor, who had been treating her disrespectfully. But she knew that every time she spoke with him she got so fearful she started crying. So what we planned was that when she went to see him, she would control three things:

- First, she would bring a glass of water with her. You may not know this trick, but drinking water is a great way to control your tears. For some reason it works.

- Second, she would sit close to the door, in case she decided she wanted to leave.

- Third, she would have an exit line ready. You'll read about exit lines next.

7. Prepare Your Exit Line

I've been speaking at conferences for women for several years, and when I explain that they absolutely need to have an exit line to navigate life, and I demonstrate it, their eyes go wide open, jaws drop, and I can tell they're having an "aha" moment. And based on what they write in their evaluations at the end of the day, I can assure you that teaching them about exit lines is one of my best sellers.

The Oxford dictionary definition of an *exit line* is, "A line spoken by an actor immediately before leaving the stage." That's where the name comes from.

You must have it memorized and well-rehearsed (like an actress) so that when necessary, you can deliver it automatically and without thinking. And then you leave the stage.

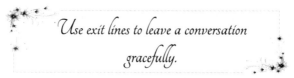

Use exit lines to leave a conversation gracefully.

I'll share with you one of the two exit lines I can deliver with my eyes closed, but remember to make your own: one that fits your style.

These are the three parts of my exit line:

1. I hear you <insert here the other person's name>.
2. I need some time to think about what you've said.
3. Let's resume this conversation <insert here when you propose to resume the conversation, such as "first thing tomorrow morning">.

Depending on the circumstances and who the other person is, you may choose a less firm and more collaborative approach: How about we resume this conversation <say when>?

What makes an exit line effective is your ability to use it *before* a conflict escalates.

There was a period of time when I was traveling too much, delivering speeches nationwide. For a few months I rarely stepped foot at home. My boyfriend back then was a very understanding and empathic man, but there was one day when he started complaining about all my traveling.

We were having this phone conversation when he was coming at me with things like, "I don't think you really care about us, because you never have time for me," or "Your job is the only thing that matters to you and I just get the leftovers."

I started getting hot (no, it was not a hot flash, thank you very much). I don't know about you, but I start feeling my body temperature rise when I start getting upset. The more he spoke, the more my internal voice was telling me, "How dare he! How inconsiderate of him! Like he doesn't know *I have to* work to support my family, and not because I love being on the road 12 hours a day. Why doesn't he help me instead of blaming me?"

That's where I was. The good thing is that I realized if I said what I was thinking, I was likely going to regret it later. He was just expressing his frustration, but I was feeling attacked and my natural reaction was to defend myself. And that's a losing proposition. So I pulled my exit line from my sleeve and delivered it in a neutral voice. "I hear you. I need some time to think about what you've said though. How about we resume our conversation after dinner?" Silence. More silence.

Then he said, "Do I have a choice?"

And I replied, "No," and I shut up again.

He said, "Okay then. Bye." And we hung up.

I forgot about the issue, because I had a lot of work to do. I didn't need the time to think, quite frankly, but to calm down and approach our next conversation in a less emotional way.

Before dinner he called me back. We had agreed on resuming after dinner, so it surprised me, but I answered his call anyway.

Me:	"Hello?"
Him:	"I'm sorry for what I said before. I was being inconsiderate. I know you work hard, and I know why you do it. I apologize."

I couldn't believe it! The "conflict" had resolved itself! I'm not saying you should avoid conflicts and let them solve themselves. No, no, no. But sometimes space gives you and the other person time to think.

8. Decide Your Stance

Do you think it's a good idea to assume different "behavior styles," or highlight certain emotions or attitudes depending on the circumstances? I do.

I'm not talking about being fake, or dishonest—I'm talking about being flexible and adapting to the circumstances.

Kind of like "dressing for the occasion," if you will.

Yesterday I attended a personal safety class. You know, those classes mostly attended by women where an expert (usually someone who is a black belt of some sort) teaches basic techniques to defend yourself from a physical attack and avoid being kidnapped by a bad guy. It was fantastic, and I think every woman should attend one, by the way.

The instructor told us about a woman who reacted to an attack in a very unusual way: she dropped to the floor and started eating grass. Eating grass for heaven's sake! The attacker backed off like, "Whoa!" I bet no attacker would have been prepared for that. He was so shocked that he left. I can understand how pretending to be crazy would discourage a kidnapper from picking you, when he can easily go pick another victim.

What this woman did was brilliant, don't you think? The instructor asked all of us, "Those of you who are mothers, what would you tell your daughter to do to ensure she gets back home safe every night?" The answer was unanimous "Anything!"

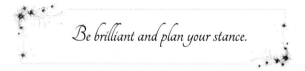

Be brilliant and plan your stance.

The takeaway from this story is not that you should eat grass. The takeaway is that if you don't consciously decide your psychological stance, the circumstances will decide it for you, and that may not be in your best interest. She decided ahead of time to act crazy if she was ever attacked, and it worked.

There will be circumstances when you want to be sincerely apologetic, a bit arrogant, cheerful, or a bit somber, and there will be other cases where that same behavior would backfire.

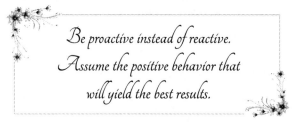

Be proactive instead of reactive.
Assume the positive behavior that
will yield the best results.

Let's play. I'll give you a few scenarios[7], and some potential psychological stances for you to pick the one(s) you think would be appropriate for the circumstances described. Then I'll give you the answers. Ready?

To ask for a raise be:

☐ Guilty

☐ Humble and subservient

☐ Chatty

☐ Decisive and confident

To refuse an assignment be:

☐ Arrogant

☐ Cynical

☐ Eager to take others in the future

☐ Disappointed but firm

To ask a peer to stop gossiping:

☐ In disbelief at their unprofessional behavior

☐ Calm

☐ Mildly offended

☐ Wounded

To deal with a client who's angry with your team:

☐ Concerned

☐ Regretful

☐ Apologetic

☐ Defensive

Answers:

- To ask for a raise be decisive and confident.

- To refuse an assignment show a bit of disappointment but eagerness to participate in future projects.

- With that co-worker who has been gossiping about you be mildly offended and in disbelief at her unprofessional behavior, but calm and unemotional.

- Finally, with the client be concerned and regretful, but neither apologetic nor defensive.

Coming up with an exhaustive list of scenarios would be impossible. Let's summarize it this way instead: just as you plan your attire and accessories for different types of events (a gala, a funeral, a dance club, a lunch with girlfriends in the summer), you need to plan before a difficult conversation.

Allow me to stretch the clothing analogy a little bit. There are some nicer things you always wear, regardless of the specifics of the occasion, right? Well, for difficult conversations those will be your positive attitude and your problem solving mindset. Don't leave home without them.

It's up to you to do whatever it takes to ensure you'll be prepared when the time comes.

9. Raise Your Confidence

You will have a script and be prepared with what to say, but it's also important for you to prepare psychologically. Yogi Berra once said, "Baseball is 90 percent mental and the other half is physical." Well, he might as well have been referring to confidence. Being confident is not only 90 percent mental—but it's also essential.

In order to be confident, first you need to see things from the other person's perspective. Or to at least try. Ask yourself questions such as, "Why does he think that?" "Why does he feel that way?" "What impression am I giving that would make him think that?" "Are there any external factors that make this worse in her mind?" And perhaps the toughest one, "Could she be acting this way as a reaction to something I do (or I did)?" Looking at ourselves in a mirror tends to be a good starting point.

I'm not recommending that you believe you *know* the other person's intentions without first asking her. No, no, no. What I'm advocating is that you think of possible scenarios (within reason), do your homework, and then go have the conversation.

Too often we go into difficult conversations with no idea where the other person is coming from and we are less confident.

You should know the other person's point of view so well that you could argue for it.

You will have more empathy for the other person and therefore have more of an *everyone-wins* focus rather than a *me-me-me* focus if you know the other side. If you don't, consider scheduling a conversation to find out *first*, and only afterwards schedule the *real* difficult conversation.

The second part of being confident is looking the part. You don't have to dress up but you need to be in clothes you are comfortable wearing while dressing appropriately for the atmosphere.

If you're physically uncomfortable, your body language will show it, even without your awareness, and if the other person perceives a bit of discomfort she may think it is about *her*. (Remember, we tend to make things about ourselves, like when we see a traffic accident on our way to work and we think, "Oh, great! Now I'm going to be late for the meeting! Why did this have to happen *to me* today!")

If you have a particular piece of jewelry that makes you feel good, wear it. I like to wear my favorite perfume which makes me feel more confident. Of course we are not really talking about extrinsic things here. This is about how these extrinsic things make you feel. Feel your best!

Picture a confident woman in your mind. What does she look like? Stop reading for a few minutes and think of your answer—grab pen and paper and write it down if you can. It's okay, I'll wait. I see your list doesn't include "beautiful."

> *A confident woman doesn't have to be beautiful in the eyes of the world, but she does have to look like she believes she's beautiful.*

Let me explain. A confident woman will be smiling, her head will be up, her shoulders will be back, she will have good eye contact, and she will walk with purpose. These are the same things that an incredibly beautiful woman will do. Picture a model. There is no way she is walking with her head down. If you aren't feeling it, no problem. Just act like you feel it!

When you assume a powerful posture (make yourself big and have an open body language) you increase your level of testosterone (and be more open to running risks) and decrease your level of cortisol (and reduce your stress). Harvard social psychologist Amy Cuddy recommends five minutes of standing like *Wonder Woman* before going into a job interview! Hands on hips, feet wide apart, shoulders back, staring confidently forward.

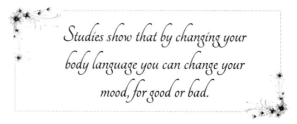

Studies show that by changing your body language you can change your mood, for good or bad.

"No way I'm doing that!" You may be thinking. "People will think I'm a nutcase if I stand five minutes like *Wonder Woman* outside our CEO's office before going into a difficult conversation with him!" I agree, I agree, calm down. Who said it had to be in public? Go to the restroom and do it. And while you do it, remember Amy Cuddy's tagline: Fake it til you *become* it.[8] Actually, go to the restroom right now and try this. You are already in the restroom? Oh, okay. (Me too.)

Practice confidence the next time you go shopping. You have a list of what a confident woman looks like, now put it to use. Stroll through the aisles at the grocery store with your head up and walk with purpose. When you see another person, give her a smile and say, "Hello," or make some other comment. If you are like me, you tend to follow people around the store unintentionally. Once I say hello the first time I say something like, "I'm stalking you," or "I'm following you," but you may not want to be that out there. Instead you can say, "Well, hello again," or you can just smile.

10. Prepare Your Script Using the NO FEAR™ Method

In the next chapter I'll explain and illustrate each one of the components of this method. For now, I'll just give you some reasons why having a script is a good idea.

Benefits of Scripting

- It ensures that you don't use ambiguous, hurtful, or inappropriate words.
- It ensures that you deliver all the important elements you need to say.
- It helps you stay focused.
- It prevents you from rambling.
- It prevents you from chickening out.

Your script will give you general direction. You know what they say, "if you don't know where you are going, you might not get there." While a script is good and helps you to prepare, be careful not to over prepare (control your perfectionism and your paralysis by analysis.)

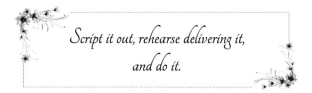

Script it out, rehearse delivering it, and do it.

The more you use the NO FEAR™ method the better you'll get at creating scripts fast. The script may sound daunting, but it really isn't. You can do it on the first try and you'll only get better with practice.

Why Rehearsing Is so Important

When delivering a speech or a presentation, some people prefer to "wing it," while others rehearse over and over. It may be a matter of personal preference, and even whether you have the improvisation skills.

You want to improve your ability to deal with difficult conversations, and that, my friend, is an indication that you will benefit from rehearsing your script before you deliver it.

One of the main reasons to do so is it helps you memorize part of it. You don't want to sound like a robot, but you want to commit certain important words and phrases to memory to ensure that you don't forget them.

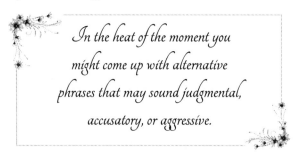

In the heat of the moment you might come up with alternative phrases that may sound judgmental, accusatory, or aggressive.

If you have been avoiding difficult conversations, you may feel uncomfortable with the NO FEAR™ script when you start using it. Over time it will become second nature and you'll be able to deliver it, as I do, automatically adapted to every situation on the spot. But the first time you'll need to hear yourself saying it so you can own it, adapt it to your style, and feel natural delivering it.

A second reason to rehearse is that you want to fine tune the nonverbal communication that goes with it: your tone of voice, your speed, and even your body language.

The same speech can sound too passive, too aggressive, or just right depending on how you deliver it.

What Did You Learn?

Take some time to process what you read. Write a few notes. What did you learn in this chapter that you will use in your next difficult conversation? How can you feel more confident? What have you done in the past to look and feel more confident? What can you do to feel more confident in the future? How can you control your environment? What's your exit line?

Your Preparation Checklist

Make copies of the preparation checklist I've included on the next page, and use one whenever you're preparing for a difficult conversation. (You'll fill your NO FEAR™ script after having read chapter four.)

☐ What's the **cost** vs. the **benefit** of this conversation?

_____

☐ My **objective** is:

_____

☐ My **reserve** value is:

_____

☐ I'm assuming **positive** intent. A positive outcome will be:

_____

☐ My **plan B** is:

_____

☐ I've planned my **environment** this way:

_____

☐ This is my **exit line**:

_____

☐ My **stance** will be:

_____

☐ To raise my **confidence** I have/I will:

_____

☐ This is my NO FEAR™ **script:**

_____

_____

_____

_____

CHAPTER FOUR

THE NO FEAR™ METHOD

Now I'm going to give you a way to remember how to have a difficult conversation when the time comes. And it will come!

It's called the NO FEAR™ method. NO FEAR™ is an acronym for the elements of the script you'll prepare *before* and deliver *during* the difficult conversation to start the dialogue with the other party. The acronym stands for:

N Nothing (Nothing comes before the objective)
O Objective

F Facts
E Effect
A Acknowledge
R Request

NO FEAR™ is easy to remember, and when you invoke it you will remember right then and there that *even if you feel afraid, you do not need to show it.*

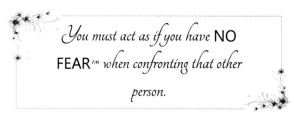

You must act as if you have NO FEAR™ *when confronting that other person.*

Think of yourself as a fighter pilot. Fighter pilots are recruited because they're tough and they don't scare easily. They may have to live through things that would terrify even the most rugged personalities. When called into action they have to *act as if they're not afraid.* Do you think they get a bottle of anxiety pills to swallow before heading into a mission so they'll be relaxed? Heck, no. Or do they practice yoga in their planes before critical moments? Not really.

They are trained to behave fearlessly. Their trainers point the plane straight for the ground until the trainee is in terror, and the trainee then learns to pull up even when terrified.[1]

If they can, you can too, so pull up!

The N in NO FEAR™ Stands for Nothing and the O Stands for Objective

It's that simple: N stands for *Nothing,* O stands for *Objective,* and *Nothing* comes before your *Objective.*

The F in NO FEAR™ is for Facts

Those of us who are used to expressing opinions and feelings more than facts will need practice to develop the skill of "speaking like a journalist."

> One of the first things you'll do in your conversation is state specific, unbiased, and recent instances of the behavior that you want eliminated.

This will make it clear what you want to talk about with the other person.

Here are some good examples:

- Sweetie, again last night you finished your dinner and immediately got up to go watch the game leaving your dishes on the table . . .

- Ike, just like last week, today at the department meeting you started talking over me when I was reporting on my progress . . .

- Pippa, yesterday after lunch when you were in the kitchen chatting with Rafaela, I overheard you telling her that you think I'm having an affair with Lucas . . .

Here are some *bad* examples and the reasons:

- Honey, about a year ago, one night when we were talking about redecorating the house, you called me lazy for no reason . . . (It's not recent. You can't expect people to remember.)

- Filbert, you always talk over me! (Vague and absolute. There's no such thing as "always." You must avoid using absolutes. Be specific.)

- You don't like me. That's why you enjoy embarrassing me in public. (You don't know what the other person thinks, likes, wants, etc. You need to focus on facts, not on opinions.)

- Sidra, at the office party yesterday, your attire was not professional. (Vague and subjective. What makes you think she understands and agrees on your concept of "professional"?)

- Elmer, yesterday you came to the office late, your tie was dirty, you didn't call *The Carrot Group* as you said you would, you . . . (Whoa whoa—just one thing at a time.)

A good way to ensure that you are sticking to the facts is to ask yourself two questions:

1. If I were an external person who wasn't there and had no idea of the background, would I understand what I'm saying?
2. Is this what I'd say if I were a reporter narrating an event? Reporters aren't supposed to interject their opinions, assumptions, or ideas. They should just explain what happened in a neutral, and clear manner.

In other words "just the facts ma'am." All you're doing is refreshing the other person's memory. Bringing him or her to the scene of the crime, so to speak. You're not complaining, interpreting, or solving anything.

The E in NO FEAR™ is for Effect

If you think people are aware of the effect of their behavior on others, think again.

Since people are often not aware of their effect on others, the second line of your script is designed to help them understand. You'll focus on *how* the behavior you described in the previous statement is negatively affecting you, them, your family, your team, your organization, or even the whales in New Zealand (Where the heck is New Zealand anyway?)

Sometimes the mere action of explaining this will have them say, "Oh, I hadn't thought of that, I'm sorry—I won't do it again." And then your mission is accomplished.

Here's an example. Not long after Susan and I (Sofia) had become business partners, she told me she wanted to talk to me about something. Here's kind of how the dialogue developed:

Susan: Sofia, when you say 'Oh, my God' without meaning to talk to God or about God, it makes me uncomfortable. I'm a Christian and I interpret that as using the Lord's name in vain.

Sofia: Oh, I'm so sorry! I wasn't aware I was doing that! As English is my second language, I sometimes pick phrases and repeat them without further thought. If it bothers you I will do my best to avoid doing it again. Thank you for explaining that to me.

Done. Problem solved. Susan didn't even need to finish her script. I was seriously not aware that my behavior was having any effect on her, and it was just ignorance. I felt really bad to know that I had been—unknowingly—potentially offending other people, including in my workshops, and I was very grateful to her.

Her prompt conversation opened up dialogue, so I explained to her that when I had just immigrated to the U.S., I used to use inappropriate words, such as afro-American or Oriental to refer to ethnic groups.

When I confessed this Susan went, "Oh, no!" She was shocked. But then I explained that as soon as nice co-workers clarified that an afro was a hairstyle from the 60s and Oriental was a rug (which I didn't know!) I understood why what I was doing was incorrect, so I immediately started working on fixing it.

One last note. Had Susan thought, "Well, since she knows I'm Christian she should know better and not do that!" we would have missed a great opportunity to open up a dialogue and understand each other better, which in turn strengthened us as a team.

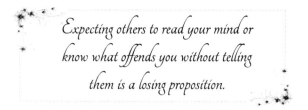

Expecting others to read your mind or know what offends you without telling them is a losing proposition.

As you read in the introduction, Susan did not start out as someone who automatically was comfortable with difficult conversations. The word "comfortable" may not be totally accurate because it may never get completely comfortable when dealing with people's feelings, but it does get easier. With some practice, and when you internalize the NO FEAR™ technique to deal with difficult conversations, you'll learn to do it in a way that comes out more naturally.

I also wanted to use this example to emphasize two other concepts I've covered elsewhere: First, she assumed positive intent. She opened up dialogue to hear my side of the story before assuming I was being intentionally disrespectful or inconsiderate. Second, I use this example to illustrate how the effect of having these conversations with a problem-solving attitude actually improves relationships. I rest my case.

The A in NO FEAR™ is for Acknowledge

The *Acknowledge* part is when you show you're compassionate and understanding. Have you heard that you catch more flies with honey? You're not the enemy, you just have a request to make, and that's all.

> *Acknowledging the person, his ideas, and even his right to see things differently than you shows respect.*

There are a couple of things you can do here: either throw him a bone or acknowledge his right to disagree. Let's discuss each option.

Your first alternative is to throw the other person a bone. This means giving a little praise or recognition. This is important in order to keep the conversation as positive as possible, but also to show that not everything about the other party is negative in your opinion. It's kind of like when you give feedback to a direct report—you don't only focus on the areas to improve, do you?

This is also like a peace offering; it shows good faith, and may diffuse the other person's defensiveness. This is also your chance to show understanding, empathy, or respect.

I had someone attending one of my public workshops once ask me, "What if I can't find anything good to say about the other person?" I have a few answers for that:

- Perhaps you didn't prepare enough.

- Perhaps you're still negatively emotionally charged and need to cool off before proceeding with this process.

- Perhaps you need to reconsider, because research shows that if you don't like someone, chances are they won't like you back. Reciprocation has been studied extensively by experts, and that's how it works.[2] This will make reaching an agreement harder, so can you get yourself to try hard and find something you may like about this person and focus on it? Perhaps he's a jerk sometimes, but you know he volunteers every weekend. Perhaps she's rude at work, but you know she's a good mom.

Your second option is just to acknowledge the other person's right to disagree with you. I'll give you a couple of examples, but let's put them into context by describing the F (Facts) and E (Effect) of our script which came before the A (Acknowledgement):

(F) Facts: Imelda, yesterday you came in at 8:15, the day before at 8:30, and on Monday at 8:45. Clients start coming in at 8:00, and when you're not on time I'm the one who's been assigned to cover the door for you.

(E) Effect: Covering for you interrupts my work, so I'm getting behind.

(A) Acknowledge: Here are some ideas:

- I understand with this weather the traffic has been heavier.
- I know you're late because you're dropping your kids at school (you're such a good mom!)
- I appreciate that you have always been on time before.
- I know what a great receptionist you are.
- I realize you may have not thought how this is impacting me.

And, there are a number of other options that may fit your circumstance. Notice that I didn't go overboard in my examples. Here is an example of saying too much in this area:

Imelda, I understand that you have to take your children to school. I love that you always put your children first and I think you are a really great mom. I wish every mom was like you. I bet you even make them breakfast! How did you have time for all that anyway? You are just so awesome!

Maybe people don't go that far overboard, but you probably know what I mean. In the past, I have been guilty of this because I was just so uncomfortable that I didn't know what to say. I have learned that the *(A) Acknowledge* part needs to be concise and to the point and going on and on can actually defeat your purpose. If you go overboard, the other person will see you as weak and you will become ineffective.

The R in NO FEAR™ is for Request

Your request is what you want the other person to start or stop doing. This is like the main course. Everything else was an appetizer. The request has to be *well thought out, realistic, nonsubjective, and measurable.* And of course it has to be stated clearly.

> *Make a behavioral request. This means that you need to describe the specific behavior you want to see.*

Realistic

I said before that you can't ask people to change something they can't change, but it's worth repeating. (Well, you can ask, but it's a waste of time.) You can't ask someone to be less boring, for instance. However, you can ask the other person for a *behavior* that would make him less boring in your eyes, maybe that he tries something that you consider fun such as riding bikes on a trail or listening to a local band you like.

Nonsubjective

Nonsubjective means "undistorted by emotion or personal bias." Asking someone to be "more romantic" is subjective, not neutral, which means that each person interprets it differently. However, you can ask him to give you flowers, a poem, or jewelry for your birthday instead of kitchen appliances (seriously?)

You can't ask someone to dress more "professionally," but you can ask her to abide by the company's dress code (which should be impartial, fair-minded, and clear.)

In my workshops I pair up the women to practice having difficult conversations. I always pick a pair and give one of them a difficult topic, "Find a way to tell her the girls are out." (Then I stand there a moment until they get it.) They laugh and then come up with all kinds of creative ways to get the other woman to cover up her cleavage. Here's an example of how women have handled the topic:

(N) Nothing:	Nothing should come before your objective.
(O) Objective:	To have her dress "more professionally."
(F) Facts:	"I notice that you wear low-cut blouses."
(E) Effect:	"This makes it difficult for people to concentrate."
(A) Acknowledgement:	"You are a great asset to the company."
(R) Request:	"So please wear a camisole when you come to work."

Measurable

I never learned how to cook spaghetti from my grandma because her explanations were not measurable: "Boil water," "Add a little bit of salt. Not too much or it will be salty," "Leave the pasta in there until it's not too hard but not too soft either." The first time I was able to cook pasta was when I read a recipe that taught me what to do in measurable terms: "Boil *six cups* of water," "Add *two teaspoons* of salt," "When the water starts to boil, add the pasta, and leave it there *12-15 minutes*." Ah, now I knew what to do!

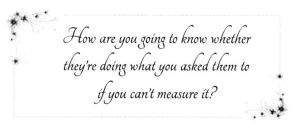

How are you going to know whether they're doing what you asked them to if you can't measure it?

You can't ask someone to get to work earlier, for instance, because you can't measure *earlier*. But you can ask him to be at his desk at 8:00 a.m. ready to work.

Don't ask your spouse to go on romantic dates with you "more often," because "more often" may mean something different to each of you. That's the same reason why "several times a month," or "as soon as possible," or "as much as we can" are not clear enough. Instead, say "once a week" for instance.

Using numbers makes what you want measurable and ensures both sides are on the same page. There's no way "once a week" means different things to different people. And if you want to be more specific and say "on Friday or Saturday" that's even better (as long as you're open to negotiating and not imposing rigid guidelines.)

Behavioral

Don't ask for a value, a belief, or an ideal. For instance, you can't ask someone to be respectful. Respect is a value (values are things that we consider valuable).

Our values guide our behavior, but nobody can ask another person to change a value. You can't ask someone to be respectful. But you can ask a person to change how they *act*.

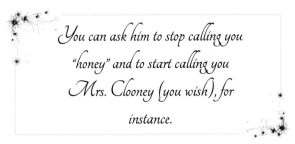

You can ask him to stop calling you "honey" and to start calling you Mrs. Clooney (you wish), for instance.

Here are some examples:

- I'd prefer it if you called us to see what our plans are instead of dropping by unexpectedly.

- I'd prefer that next time you need to give me negative feedback you do it in private.

- I'd prefer that whenever something about me bothers you, you tell me directly instead of telling someone else.

These are behavioral requests because you're not asking others to change their feelings or beliefs, but to change something they *do*.

In those examples I used the words "I prefer" to start each request, but you can pick whichever words fit your style. You could say, for instance, "In the future please . . ." Just don't be wordy, don't beat around the bush, and make sure you use decisive language.

Be Positive

Using positive language makes your requests easier to understand and makes you look like a positive person, so try to phrase your requests in positive terms.

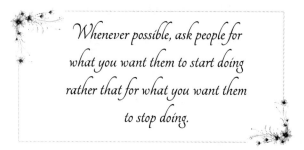

Whenever possible, ask people for what you want them to start doing rather that for what you want them to stop doing.

This takes practice, but it's not hard. For instance, instead of saying, "Don't leave your desk a mess at the end of the day," say "Please pick up your desk before leaving for the day."

Here are a few examples for you to practice. Turn these requests into positive ones:

- You want your friend to stop complaining to you about another friend and start

  _____.

- You want your co-worker to stop leaving the copier without paper and start

  _____.

- You want your co-worker to stop heating fish in the microwave. You will ask him to start _____.

- You want your son to stop coming home after midnight. You will ask him to _____.

- You want your sister to start _____ instead of discussing your private things with your mother.

You'll enjoy the effects of people starting to perceive you more as a positive person (and actually like you more.)

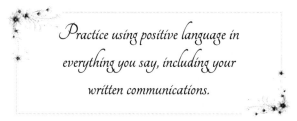

Practice using positive language in everything you say, including your written communications.

Let's Prepare Your Script

Let's script the first conversation you want to tackle. Get yourself a piece of paper, a quiet area to work, and perhaps your favorite drink. If music helps you focus go ahead and play some. Now fill the following information about your upcoming difficult conversation:

(N) Nothing: Remind yourself that *Nothing* will come before your *Objective*.

(O) Objective: Describe your objective(s). Do it concisely.

(F) Facts: Describe a specific instance of the behavior you want to change. (Two is fine.)

(E) Effect: How is this behavior impacting others?

(A) Acknowledge: Throw the other person a bone!

(R) Request: Be specific when describing the behavior you want to see.

How Did It Go?

These are the most common mistakes I see women make when they use NO FEAR.™ If you made them in your script, no worries, this is why we review it before actually using it in the conversation.

Check the areas you need to work on:

☐ I used absolute words, such as "always," "never," etc.

☐ I used vague words.

☐ I used phrases that could be considered accusatory, such as "You are inconsiderate" or "You don't care" instead of describing the behavior that bothers me.

☐ I didn't explain the impact of their actions, preferably not only on me but also on others and on our organization.

☐ I forgot to say something positive.

☐ I didn't include a specific, clear, behavioral request. (Believe it or not, this is where people struggle. You need to explain to the other person what you're asking.)

What Did You Learn?

Take some time to process what you read. What did you learn in this chapter? What do you like about the NO FEAR™ script? What can you do to improve your communication skills? What mistakes have you made in the past (no, I am not talking about that bikini wax you got last summer), such as not using factual language, not making a specific request, or asking for something that was not realistic?

CHAPTER FIVE

THE MUST-HAVE ELEMENTS OF YOUR CONVERSATION

A speech, a presentation, or a business document with good structure has three parts:

1. Introduction / Attention grabber
2. Body / Content of the message
3. Conclusion / Call to action

A difficult conversation also needs these three because each part accomplishes a specific purpose for you to reach your desired results.

We'll start this chapter with a sample conversation so you can see the three parts "in action." Then we'll discuss the specifics and you'll be able to get the whole picture.

Sample Conversation

You:	"Hi Vita. There's something I'd like to talk to you about. It shouldn't take more than ten minutes. Is this a good time?"
Vita:	"Sure, just gimme a minute to send this email and I'll be right with you. Have a seat."
You:	"Thanks."
Vita:	"Okay, I'm ready. What's going on?"
You:	
Facts:	"Well, Vita, yesterday at the weekly meeting you presented the idea I had shared with you about the research for the ABC project by saying, 'I think that we should outsource the research!' That implies outsourcing is *your* idea. (Don't pause, go on.)
Effect:	When I heard that, I felt disappointed. I came to clarify this because I don't want this to negatively impact our trust and our work as a team. (Keep going, you're doing great. Keep eye contact.)
Acknowledgement:	I understand that you may have done this unintentionally, and I like that you appreciate my idea, however . . .

Request: I'm here to ask you to go talk to our boss
and tell him that it was *my* idea. Would
you be able to do it before or after lunch
today? (Assume she will.)

<Silence>

Vita may apologize, agree, get defensive, attack, or any
other reaction, and you may use some of the recommendations
we'll share in this section to respond. At some point, however,
the dialogue will wind down, and then it will be time to wrap up.
Let's look at two options.

Option A: You didn't reach an agreement.

You: "It's unfortunate that it seems we can't come
to an agreement."

Option B: You did reach an agreement:

You: "I knew you'd understand, thank you. I appreciate you talking to Joe after lunch about
my outsourcing idea."

Vita: "You're welcome."

You: "I'd better go back to work now."

Notice how in option B your first line is designed to
confirm the important agreements you reached without sounding condescending.

Follow up with her the next day to see how it went.
You don't need to tell her that you will, or when will
you do it. It's your follow up so do it when it's more
convenient for you. Just don't take what I just said as
an excuse to procrastinate or avoid doing it.

Introduction

Avoid "Previews"

Do you remember when you were preparing for the conversation you considered (based on the specific circumstances and on the other party) whether to make an appointment or just stop by?

If the person can't have the conversation when you stop by (with or without an appointment), don't give the details of your script. Save it for the real deal. Here's how to handle it:

You:	"Hi Vita. Do you have ten minutes to spare for me now?"
Vita:	"What is it you want to talk to me about?"
You:	"I'd like to discuss it when you have time."
Vita:	(She will say if she has time or not.)
You:	(If she doesn't) "I have my calendar, can we set up an appointment soon?"
Vita:	"Yes, but I need to know what this is about before I'll set up the appointment." (Now you understand she feels she has to know.)
You:	"Sure, it's about the ABC project."

What you have done is let her know the overall topic but you have not revealed your issue.

Your words and tone need to express calmness so she is not put on the defensive.

If she is on the defensive prior to your conversation, she is more likely to act tense and the discussion may be more difficult than it needs to be.

There is nothing wrong with telling her what this is about, and it's not a matter of being mysterious. It's a matter of control. It's *your* conversation, so it should be you who decides when and how you disclose what you want.

Make the Introduction Brief and Direct

To help you stay focused, start with an introduction that is brief and direct.

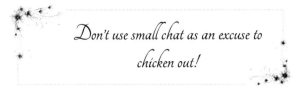

Don't use small chat as an excuse to chicken out!

You have already given her a time estimate because you don't want her to stand up in the middle of your script and say, "Oh, I gotta go!" Stick to your time estimate if possible. Otherwise the other person will likely not give you another "ten minutes" next time knowing it's really going to be half an hour.

Keep in mind that I'm using ten minutes as an example. Some conversations will take two minutes and others will require a full hour. Try to estimate how much time you need based on the complexity of the issue and your knowledge of the other person. Don't make it too long because people lose focus or get tired.

All that being said, I'd try to set a time limit of 15 to 20 minutes. No one wants to talk about their tardiness, for example, for an hour. However, if it is a complex issue you have been putting off, twenty minutes may not cut it either.

When you give your time estimate you may suggest that if you both agree you need more time you can schedule a follow up appointment.

The Body

Let Your Objective Guide You

Your objective needs to be on your mind the entire time of the conversation. Remind yourself of the NO part of the NO FEAR™ method to make sure you do what you came to do in spite of your fears or how others may try to take you off course. *(N) Nothing* should come before your *(O) Objective.* State your objective often during the conversation, but do it in silence, though, or you may seem a little off.

Deliver Your Script and Dialogue

Then you deliver your script without letting the other person interrupt you.

Then, and only then, you stop talking and listen attentively, trying to understand what is being said and the emotions behind the words.

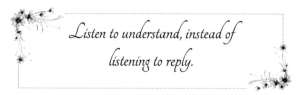

Listen to understand, instead of listening to reply.

Ask open ended questions until you feel comfortable that you *really* understand the other person's perspective. Open ended questions are the kind that can't be answered with just a yes or a no. The answer requires more than one or two words. Open questions usually start with the word why. My friend Rick just says, "Tell me more," which allows the other person to express themselves freely and say things you might not have thought of asking.

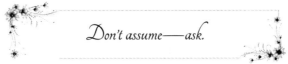

Don't assume—ask.

Collaborating respectfully in order to find a mutually agreeable solution is key. You'll need to open your mind and separate the problem from the person so you can be as creative as possible when seeking a joint solution.

Keep the conversation going until you reach an agreement, even if the agreement is that you disagree on the matter. Don't drag the conversation out more than necessary, don't repeat yourself, and don't give up too soon.

The Conclusion

When You Don't Agree

You're going to try your best to reach an everybody-wins solution, but in real life it's not always possible despite your best intentions.

> *If you didn't reach an agreement*
> *move to your plan B.*

Whether you tell the other party what you intend to do after the conversation or not is a matter of personal preference. I prefer not to say what I plan to do unless there's a compelling reason. It may not even be her business, so why give her ammunition to hurt me?

For instance, in the previous example, I wouldn't let Vita know that I will inform our supervisor. If she still believes (or pretends that she believes) it was *her* idea, she may well beat me to our supervisor's office and tell him *first* that it was *her* idea. Do you see the problem? By the time I talk to our boss he may already be predisposed because he heard Vita's version first.

When You Agree

The previous example illustrates three important functions of the conclusion:

1. It summarizes and **confirms** the agreement. This avoids misunderstandings in the future ("Wait a minute, I never said I would!")

2. It states a **deadline** for its completion.

3. It states when and how you will **follow up**.

Summarizing and confirming the **agreement** is indispensable, because it avoids misunderstandings in the future ("Wait a minute, I never said I would!")

Agreeing on a **deadline** is imperative. You want to know when this will be done so you can follow up and act accordingly (whether it was done or not). Depending on your style you will state the deadline matter-of-factly ("I want to ask you to talk to our supervisor this week"), or you'll give them some power by asking them to choose between one of two options ("Do you want me to go with you or do you prefer to go alone?") I like the second choice, just because I like to have options.

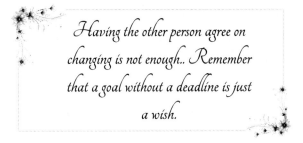

Having the other person agree on changing is not enough.. Remember that a goal without a deadline is just a wish.

Finally, letting the other person know when and how you will **follow up** is critical. This confirms accountability and commitment. It also allows the other person to throw one last objection, if they have one, while you can still address and diffuse it.

Stick to Your Word on the Time

As previously mentioned, staying on time is important. I have experienced situations where I am in the conclusion portion and ready to end it at the time I stated. However, the person wants to go on and discuss it more. I simply say something like, "We are at the ten-minute mark now. I have more time if you'd like to discuss this further or we can make another appointment." This way the ball is in her court and I have stuck to my word.

End in a Pleasant Tone

If you reached an agreement, deliver the conclusion on a friendly tone. "I'm glad we reached an agreement, I knew we would."

If you didn't come to an agreement, deliver the conclusion in a neutral tone, but still thank the other person for his or her time. You are in control of this (remember you have a plan B?) so don't lose your cool, and don't show any negativity.

If you're frustrated or having any other negative emotion, go cry in the bathroom, take a walk, meditate, or hit the punching bag you have in your closet (the one with the person's picture on it—kidding), but do that in private.

What Did You Learn?

Take some time to process what you read. Write a few notes. Buy me some ice cream (did it work?) All right, let's be serious. What did you learn in this chapter that you will use in your next difficult conversation? When do you plan on having this conversation? How will you start the dialogue? How could you end on a pleasant note? I know I will end this on a pleasant note and I'll go get myself some ice cream while you ponder this chapter.

CHAPTER SIX

WHAT TO DO *DURING* THE DIFFICULT CONVERSATION

Put Your Helmet On™

*M*y friend Bob says I invented the *Put Your Helmet On™* technique. I say it was him. But since both of us have a bad memory, and we love each other, let's just say we both came up with it simultaneously. Weirder things have happened.

Here's how to use it:

1.   Read and understand the technique.

2. Explain it to someone you love, care about, and/or work with whom you may have difficult conversations in the future. You may use our saying, or adapt the idea using your own words—make it your own. That way, you are creating a "meta-language," or a *code* that the two of you understand. Codes that are clear and mutually agreed upon make communication efficient and create a sense of intimacy that helps you get into collaboration-mode.

3. In this code when one of you says to the other, "Put your helmet on,"™ you both know what he or she means is this:

I need to have a difficult conversation with you. What I have to say may not be pleasant. We may see things differently, or I may need to say something you won't like or would prefer not to hear. Still, I think it's important for me to tell you.

I will be mindful of your emotions and your right to disagree. My intention is not to judge you, criticize you, or in any way harm you. I believe that having this conversation will benefit you, me, our relationship, and/or our common endeavors.

4. Depending on your relationship with the other person you may add at the end something like, "Remember I love you," or "I do this because I appreciate our friendship," or "I value being on your team."

5. Opening up that way shows the other person you care and you come in peace. Obviously, your comments need to be genuine.

6. Then the other person can tell you when he or she has a helmet on, and will try to be more thick-skinned, take things less personally, and understand where you're coming from. You may even hear "Put your helmet on™" too!

In his video *Managing Difficult Conversations*, Dr. Fred Kofman, professor of leadership at the Argentinian University *Universidad Francisco Marroquín*, reminds us of the saying, "I don't care how much you know until I know how much you care," and adds, "you have to show the other person that you care before they will listen to what you know."[1] That's exactly what the Put Your Helmet On™ technique accomplishes.

Be Sugar, Spice, and Everything Nice

Multiple studies show that women increase their chances of a successful outcome in difficult conversations when they use a "soft style," and are penalized (by men and by other women) when they are perceived as acting aggressively.[2]

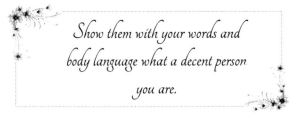

Show them with your words and body language what a decent person you are.

Oh, and before you think this recommendation is outdated, read the works cited at the end of this book and find studies conducted with men and women as young as their late teens and early twenties to confirm that my advice is totally twenty-first century. I am not suggesting you become someone you're not, however, consider you may need to soften your approach to increase your chances of getting what you want.

What's the Problem?

One of the main enemies of effective conflict resolution is our belief that, if only the other person allowed us to explain our side first and she understood it, she would agree with us and the problem would go away. In reality that's not usually the case.

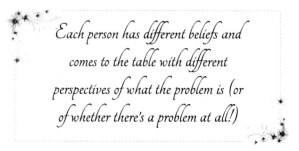

Each person has different beliefs and comes to the table with different perspectives of what the problem is (or of whether there's a problem at all!)

Start by finding out what the problem is. This sounds obvious: if you don't know what the problem is, you can't solve it. Still, most people assume that both parties know and agree on this and therefore jump into solving it without first clarifying their points of view and finding common ground.

In one of my workshops, a woman named Guinevere waited for me after it was over. She wanted to discuss her problem with me in private. She started with, "Will you help me prepare my NO FEAR™ script?" Of course I agreed.

"What's your problem?" I asked.

"My boss doesn't talk to me," she said. "I want to write a script asking her to talk to me."

"What?" I thought. It left me perplexed that a supervisor could not talk to an employee and work could get done anyway. Did they email, text, or use sign language instead? Weird. "Tell me more," I replied. (Tip: when you're totally perplexed you need to ask an open question more than ever.)

"Well," Guinevere continued, "ever since I came back from the two weeks off I took about three months ago, she avoids me. She doesn't even say good morning, and she doesn't interact with me." At this point her voice started breaking and her eyes started watering. I didn't want to pry, but I made a mental note wondering about the circumstances under which she had taken those weeks off, because that seemed to have been the event which triggered the problem.

"Why is she not talking to you?" I asked.

"I don't know," she said.

"Well, it's good that you're not assuming and are instead accepting that you don't know. That's great!" I said.

"Thank you."

"Still," I went on, "I want to know your best guess of what triggered a change in her conduct. Could it be that she didn't want you to take those weeks off? Could it be that you took them at a bad time, and left her with more work than she could handle? What's your best guess?"

That's when Guinevere opened up. "It was actually her idea that I attended an alcoholism recovery camp for two weeks. We were friends." She was clearly embarrassed to admit it, but her openness was key to solving the problem. "So I don't know why she stopped talking to me when I came back."

Do you agree with me that we don't know what the problem is? What Guinevere wanted was to "cure" the symptom rather than to diagnose the illness. "I want your help to write a NO

FEAR™ script and my request will be that she talks to me again," she had said, but at this point it's clear that she should start by writing a script requesting her boss to tell her why her behavior towards her changed after she came back from the camp.

Instead of wondering what the problem was ("Do you think it could be you who changed after the camp and she's just reacting?" "Could it be that she can't manipulate you anymore and she resents it?") what Guinevere needs to do is to set as her objective to find out her supervisor's perspective on their relationship after the camp.

Even when it sounds unlikely, it could even be the issue has nothing to do with Guinevere, but with other events that by chance happened while Guinevere was out! Trying to guess is a waste of time. You could use the old phrase my friend Traci uses on me. "Don't borrow trouble." Instead, just go and prepare your script to find out.

Focus on the Future, Not on the Past

Yes, knowing the past is important—that's why you start the conversation stating the facts that lead you to it. But you're only using what has happened in the past to provide the context for your conversation, or—in other words—to explain the cause-effect of what you want to change.

Once that's done, your primary focus needs to be in the future, because that's where the solution is. Focusing on the future is not only more practical but is also healthier for your relationship with the other party. Who cares whose fault it is? Let's move on! Who cares what either of you could have done differently? As Stephen Colbert says, "Don't cry over spilled milk. By this time tomorrow, it will be free yogurt!" Seriously, nobody can change the past, so why bother feeling bad about it instead of using positive energy to make things better?

Focusing on the future allows you to avoid statements that don't bring anything positive to the table, but that may cause resentment: "You should have told me." "Well, I didn't and I can't change the past, so why make me feel bad by saying it when there's nothing I can do about it?"

I had a friend whose mother was usually telling her what she could (or should) have done differently. She said things such as, "Too bad you didn't think of telling him not to call you again," or "You could have asked her to leave." It was her way of giving better solutions that were impossible to implement because they were in the past! (Mom, it's not you, it really is a friend.)

Being right is overrated. Do you want to be right at the expense of making the other person feel stupid, or do you want her to feel good and willing to cooperate with you which will ease your pain? (Stop arguing with me in your head. Yes, I hear you.)

Sometimes you do want that other person to feel stupid or some other negative emotion because that's what you felt! But, stop it! Just try it my way for a while and keep your thoughts to yourself and act like you don't care about being right.

> *Don't play the blame game.*
> *Remember that saying, "I should*
> *have..." is counterproductive.*
> *Move on and focus on what you*
> *can do, not on what you can't.*

Make Requests That Will Benefit Others

Over the years I have had many opportunities to remind my daughter that women don't ask for things often enough, and that she needs to ask more. And on many occasions she has shown me she has learned her lesson well, even to the point that a couple times I've regretted having taught her that lesson (when she asks me to stay at her friend's late or when a teacher allowed her to delay a test because she hadn't studied.)

Still, I was recently reminded that we sometimes forget to make requests on our own behalf (or avoid it.) My daughter was at school when one of her teachers announced a boy in her group had asked to be the president for the mock trial team (mock trial is a program created to help students acquire a working knowledge of our judicial system. They assume the roles of attorneys and witnesses in a fictional trial, and compete against other schools). My daughter had wanted to be the president too, but apparently she hadn't asked for it, and (surprise) a boy asked first.

That's when something interesting happened. One of my daughter's girlfriends raised her hand and told the teacher, "I know that Dani wants to be president too." So the teacher said, "Oh. Well, they both can be co-presidents." Not a bad solution, I think.

If that friend hadn't spoken up, my daughter would have lived with the fact that the title had already been given, and she wouldn't have said anything about it. Would you say anything *after* a promotion has already been given to one of your co-workers? Most of us would have *assumed* it was too late. How fortunate my daughter is to have a friend who didn't!

That story reminded me of something I had read in *Lean In*, Facebook COO Sheryl Sandberg's bestselling book.[3] She says women are better off if they ask for something *for someone else* rather than for themselves. They come across as less selfish, and are consistent with the widespread stereotype about women being caregivers. I'm not saying it is wrong to ask for yourself, but sometimes it may work to team up with another woman, just like many other women have.

Be Open Minded

Being rigid or judgmental is not being open minded. You have an objective and you have a reserve value (the minimum you are willing to settle for), yes, but you need to be open to adapting your strategy (and perhaps your request) based on the new information you'll acquire as the conversation progresses. Remember those who adapt survive.

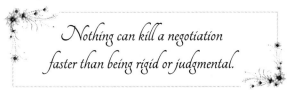

Nothing can kill a negotiation faster than being rigid or judgmental.

If you sense that you're been stuck in a topic, ask yourself, "Am I being inflexible?" (And don't give yourself a rigid answer!) It also helps to ask yourself, "What is it that I may not know?" and use the opportunity to turn your positional stance into a curious stance. Be open to the possibility that what you don't know, but what you're open to discovering, might change your point of view.

If those arguments haven't convinced you, think of this: being rigid makes you seem older. Isn't it true that younger people, in general, are more flexible?

Get rid of a few years just by being adaptable and open minded. (It's harder than anti-wrinkle cream, but cheaper!)

Be Pleasant

Start on a pleasant note and continue with it through the conclusion. Your tone needs to be neutral. Don't seem upset, but don't seem too friendly either.

Use your "pass me the butter" tone. You know, the one you'd use at dinner to, well, ask someone to pass you the butter.

Just because you're in a negotiation doesn't mean you should act formal and reserved.[4]

Sometimes you will need to make an extra effort to keep your cool and be nice despite being upset or having been offended. Just focus on your objective.

There's ample evidence women are evaluated differently than men for displaying the same behavior.

When it comes to conflict resolution, we as women, have to keep our cool in order to be viewed fairly compared to men even to a point where it seems ridiculous.

Take the results of a study on male and female leaders published by the *Journal of Personality and Social Psychology*, for instance. The researchers assembled a group of leaders of both genders. They sat them around a table, and instructed the participants to engage in a group discussion. All of them were displaying a *collaborative* attitude and analyzing different points of view *calmly*—in short, men and women alike were displaying a set of clearly *constructive* responses to conflict.

At the same time a group of naïve observers—who were the guinea pigs of this experiment—were watching. And, there was a third layer of people: the researchers, who were observing the guinea pigs observing the people having the difficult conversation. Sounds like fun, doesn't it?

Here's what the researchers found: they coded the facial expressions of the guinea pigs, and they reported that "greater levels of displeasure were evident toward female leaders." In other words, the same *constructive* pattern of behavior evoked more *negative* responses toward women.[5]

"Why be nice then?" you may be wondering. Good question. Because it's the lesser of two evils. There is evidence that the use of a *dominating* style is *more strongly negatively correlated* with perceptions of effectiveness for female than for male managers.[6] In plain English it means that, as a woman, the more dominating you behave, the less competent people may think you are.

Be decisive but pleasant.

Keep Control of the Conversation

When you are in a difficult conversation, the other person may try and take you off course. For instance, you are talking about how you'd like Julie to dress appropriately at work and she comes back and says, "Mary dresses like I do." It is easy to then begin moving the conversation to Mary instead of Julie.

Confidence helps you to stop this. You can say something like, "Right now I'd like to bring the topic back to you." Or in another circumstance, "You make a good point about that, but first let's talk about this." If you aren't confident, you are likely to let the other person drive the conversation. A confident person doesn't allow that but instead takes control which is more likely to produce the results you want.

You can use this same technique when the other person tries to turn the tables on you.

You: "Bubba, I want to ask you to be on time when we have a date."

Bubba: "Me? It's *you* who's late most of the time."

You: <Resist the temptation to defend yourself or to attack back and be like two kids that keep saying, "You!" "No, you!" "No, you *more!*">

You: "I respect that you see things that way, and I'm open to listening to what you have to say. I care about your opinion, so let's discuss *me* once we're done with this. For now, however, let's go back to the topic of this conversation: request that you're on time from now on."

In case you didn't know, you said that calmly and nicely.

Don't be afraid to sound like a broken record.

This is not a speech contest.

You showed you care about what he had to say, but you didn't let him control your conversation. You can do this as many times as needed to stay on track until you reach a conclusion.

For me it has been really hard not to defend myself immediately after I'm accused of something. My ego wants to jump in and say, "Wait a minute! That's not true!" but I don't do it because I *have seen* firsthand how it makes things worse, and how when I calm down, slow down, and stop feeling threatened I end up getting more respect. The other person usually ends up calming down too. Plus, I don't suffer from a regret-hangover.

It takes a conscious effort to realize that defending yourself won't solve the problem but will take you off track and you'll end up quarrelling and solving nothing. Breathe and remind yourself your objective. You are focused, and you're on a mission. Lose focus and you'll lose the mission.

Bring Down Defenses

Ideally, we want to put the other person at ease so he or she becomes less defensive. The more defensive she is, the more difficult the conversation will be. Your body language can help you to come across as less of a threat.

You need to show that you are open to what she has to say. Keep your arms from being crossed or resting on your hips. Instead put them to your sides without clenching your fists. Or if it feels more natural, hold something like a notebook in your hand.

Use your head to nod slightly at what she says when you agree, but do not shake your head when you disagree. Notice I said "nod slightly," not a constant nodding—you don't want to look like a bobblehead, or overly eager to please. Keep your body toward her to show that she has your full attention. Lean in a little.

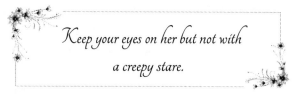

Keep your eyes on her but not with a creepy stare.

Angle your body slightly (opposite of her if she is angled) which is a more relaxed stance. Keep your knees slightly bent so you don't lock them. Notice how she is standing or sitting and slightly mirror her. If her legs are crossed, perhaps you cross at the ankles. This makes her feel more at ease because you are like her. It may sound difficult, but practice mirroring on friendly conversations and you'll see it's not that hard.

What else can you do to bring down defenses? You can go into the conversation thinking that the other person may not even see this as difficult. Oftentimes we have stress over things that turn out not to be stressful for the other person.

For instance, you may consider it difficult to ask your cubicle neighbor to lower his voice (or face in the opposite direction) when calling clients because it distracts you. You may work yourself up and get really nervous and you put it off and put it off. Then when you finally tell the person he might say, "Oh, I hadn't realized it. I know I raise my voice when I'm pumped up, but I hadn't thought how it may be distracting to others. I'll work on it."

Goodness! You wasted all that time and energy and worry for nothing! Have you heard the Mark Twain quote on worry? "I've had a lot of worries in my life, most of which never happened." That's absolutely true for me. I've had many conversations I worried about and made things worse just from worrying!

Use Your Female Assets

I'm sure you have many assets, but the ones I'll talk about here are your talent to read body language and to detect emotions.

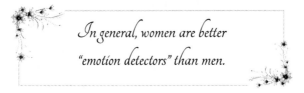

In general, women are better "emotion detectors" than men.

Judith Hall analyzed 125 studies of sensitivity to nonverbal cues and concluded that women surpass men in reading people when shown "thin slices" of behavior[7] (a few seconds of film clips).

Women have also performed better than men in studies that have asked them to identify genuine romantic couples from posed phony couples, or to discern which of two people in a photo is the other person's supervisor.[8] I know my teen nieces avoid their mom like the plague when they get home after curfew because they believe she's a human lie detector! It is really funny to see them walk into their home and chat a few minutes with their dad, but when they hear their mom's steps, they run like the wind.

Listen. No, Really. Listen.

Listening is also a great way to bring down defenses. A wall goes up when you know someone is not listening to you. Do what you can to keep the walls down. Focus on what she is saying rather than what you'll say next. This is so easy to read here, but may be hard to do. It's not actually that difficult, but it does take practice. Make a point to start doing it today—remember that effective listening is a learned skill and therefore it can be developed over time.

Here's one way to improve your listening skills: focus on the other person, not on yourself. Do that intentionally. If your attention drifts, bring it back. In her book *The Charisma Myth*, Olivia Fox Cabane quotes a 2,250-person study co-authored by Harvard psychologist Daniel Gilbert that estimated that nearly half of the average person's time was spent "mind wandering."[9] Half the time! (Wait! Is your mind wandering now?)

When you decided to confront this person you committed to being present and listening attentively, but that may change as the conversation progresses and you start falling into the temptation of planning your next move or judging her while the other person is talking. I get it.

You don't need to silence that internal voice that's talking to you all the time—just keep her under control. When you're thinking about what you'll respond the focus is on yourself and your opinions, whereas when you focus on the other's person body language, on the feelings behind her words, and on what she may be thinking, then the focus is on her. That's when true understanding may happen. What's not being said is as important as what's being said—usually even more!

Observe the other person for clues. As Yogi Berra said, "You can observe a lot by just watching." Use empathy to wonder how she may be feeling, ask her open ended questions so she can expand her explanations.

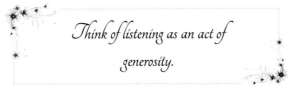

Think of listening as an act of generosity.

You are a generous person—here's your chance to show it, be a great listener. Great listening is an act of generosity.

If you look like you are listening, you have a better chance of listening (although it's not fool proof.) That goes back to the eye contact and head nodding but also includes verbal cues. You could ask a question or say, "Ah" or some other noise. If the environment is right I like to take notes. Just short little words that pop into my head of what I want to say when the other person is finished. Then I can stop thinking about what I want to say. When it's my turn, I briefly look at my list.

A technique I like to use is called the "echo." This is where you restate what the person just said in your own words with empathy.

Ludovic says, "I don't understand why your company can't get orders to me on time!"

You could say, "Ludovic, I can see you're raising a very valid concern. I am going to look into your orders right now." If he raised his voice, raise yours a touch (not yelling and not as loud as him) and sound passionate, not angry. That will bring down his defenses because he sees you as being empathetic.

Echoing can also be used to confirm agreement or set a commitment during the conclusion part of your conversation. "Okay, so we are both in agreement that we will follow up next Tuesday." Or perhaps, "Okay, thank you for talking to me and I really appreciate your willingness to try and not curse around me."

I've had "conversations" with people where I don't say hardly anything, I listen attentively, and when they leave they say things like, "I enjoyed talking with you! You are such a great conversationalist!"

I'll wrap this section up with two slices of wisdom to get you thinking. One, people's favorite sound is their own voice. Two, as Maya Angelou said, "People may not remember what you said, but they will remember how you made them feel."

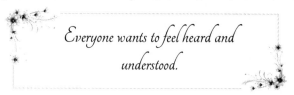

Everyone wants to feel heard and understood.

Learn to Be Silent

Listening effectively is not only giving your full attention to the other person when she's talking. It's also letting her talk in the first place! Practice being comfortable with silence. Marcus Tulius Cicero said, "Silence is one of the great arts of conversation," and while this is true during friendly dialogue, it's even more crucial during a difficult conversation.

I remember a wonderful female sales trainer I worked with many years ago. She was very polished, but she was such a fast thinker, and had so much to say, she tended to ask a second question before giving people time to answer the first one. She would say, for instance, "What do you reply when your client says your product is too expensive?" "Do you explain that it's not, or do you ask him why he thinks that?"

Sometimes she would ask more than two questions in a row! This mistake is commonly made by people who are confident about their subject matter and tend to be impatient. Remember to make a conscious effort to adapt to people who are more reflective and need more time than you to process information. Ask one question that expands possibilities, and then wait.[10]

Okay, I Tried All That and She's Still Defensive

Could it happen that after you do everything I have suggested the other person is still behaving defensively? You betcha. It could be the person you're dealing with is one of those rare (but very real) individuals that resist seeing any of their own flaws or assuming responsibility.

My mom calls them, "those who prefer to *be right* than to *do what's right*." (And believe me, *she* knows!) Some people will not admit they are wrong, period, no matter how good you are at showing empathy and at active listening. It could also be that this particular issue is sensitive to them, and they may feel psychologically threatened. The truth is that human beings are complex, and you don't know what you don't know.

Have you ever met someone that always has an excuse (that they refer to as "a reason") for what goes wrong that prevents him from having to assume responsibility? Yes, like the person that's consistently late and blames traffic, the weather, his car, etc. but never his unwillingness to plan and start driving earlier? That's what I mean.

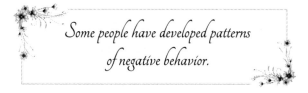

Some people have developed patterns of negative behavior.

Others may try to turn the tables on you, use excuses, deny the problem, or use any other strategy to divert attention from their faults and avoid responsibility.

Before you judge others though, just remember, once again, that you don't know what you don't know. Many years ago I briefly went out with a man, let's call him Marshall, whom hardly ever (if at all) assumed any responsibility for whatever disagreements we had. Being with Marshall was like walking on eggshells, because every small disagreement could turn life into a battlefield. Once he told me what a terrible childhood he had and how awfully abusive his mother had been, I understood better the scars that living in that nightmare had left on him. Believe me, you don't want to know. You really don't. That's when I understood why Marshall was always needing to defend himself. Under his 6'2" tough-guy façade and his deep voice there was a little boy who was shaking in fear of being inadequate.

I'm not excusing anybody from assuming responsibility, but this is where I remind you that I'm not a mental health professional, and if you aren't either then all we can be sure of is that when we confront someone we don't know what we don't know.

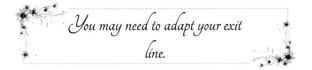

You may need to adapt your exit line.

If you find yourself needing to confront someone like this, you may want to adapt your exit line and use it. Try several times to keep him on track, to calmly listen to his side, and to explain yours in order to find a joint solution, not to prove him wrong. But if it all fails, you may say,

> "Rodolfo, I hear you. It seems that we could use a break to think over everything that has been said. I know I'd like some time to regain my composure. Let's resume our conversation tomorrow morning."

(What is he going to say? "No, I won't give you time to regain your composure?" Not likely.)

Then on the next day before resuming this particular difficult conversation, you may want to address the problem you're having when communicating. You can use the NO FEAR™ method here too:

(N) Nothing: Nothing comes before your objective.

(O) Objective: To have Rodolfo open his mind and lower his defenses. To make him feel I'm not attacking him.

(F) Facts: "Rodolfo, yesterday, when we were discussing the XYZ client issue you said things such as 'You didn't plan for it!' or 'You didn't include it in the report,' and the like. You raised your voice and repeatedly pointed at me." (At this point, resist using the same tone he used on you.)

(E) Effect: "I perceived your behavior as defensive, and I got defensive too. And then we didn't communicate effectively."

(A) Acknowledge: "I know we're both under stress and you are a very competent engineer, so..."

(R) Request: "I want to ask you to remember that I'm on your side and that I want to understand you so we can solve problems faster."

Did you notice the use of "I" language ("I perceived your behavior as defensive...")? That's assertive and non-accusatory. "You" language sounds accusatory ("You were defensive") and raises the other person's defenses immediately.

There's something else you need to be careful with: before you go around playing psychologist and blaming everyone else, it's a good idea to take a few minutes and go look at yourself in the mirror.

> *Could it be that what you don't like in her is something that you do too? Do you avoid seeing it in yourself and instead focus on him? Don't say no too fast—it's worth taking a hard look at yourself.*

I had read about this phenomenon, but like many people, I thought it applied to everyone else but me, right? Right. My "Aha!" moment happened one day when, excited, I went to tell a fellow speaker in a conference about a great success story I had just heard, and she turned to me, cold and upset, and said, "Don't talk to me when I'm counting. That's what I'm doing and you're interrupting me!" I knew she was more on the aggressive than on the passive side, but whoa, that was rude!

I was about to tell myself how that reaction was uncalled for when it hit me: I was interrupting her exactly the same way I hated when my mom interrupted me when I was writing! Sure, she expressed it in a way that was not the kindest, but it is true it's easier to see the speck in someone else's eye than the log that's in our own. Enough said.

Now, what to do if it all fails? Well, rest easy! We cover that in the next chapter.

What Did You Learn?

Take some time to process what you read. Write a few notes. What did you learn in this chapter that you will use in your next difficult conversation? Here's a checklist of things to ponder before your next difficult conversation. You don't need to write down your answers—just think about them while you're showering, gardening, styling your hair, etc. Focus on the ones that have been challenging for you. C'mon, you know which ones.

Here's Your Checklist

- [ ] Will you ask him, "Put Your Helmet On™?
- [ ] What will you do to ensure you're being sugar, spice, and everything nice?
- [ ] What's the problem?
- [ ] What will you do to ensure you're focusing on the future?
- [ ] What will you do to ensure you're being open minded?
- [ ] Have you practiced your "pass me the butter" tone?
- [ ] What will you do to keep control of the conversation?
- [ ] What will you to do to bring down defenses?
- [ ] How will you use your female assets?
- [ ] How will you improve your listening skills?
- [ ] How will you practice to become comfortable with silence?
- [ ] Who can help you with that?

CHAPTER SEVEN

KEEP YOUR EMOTIONS UNDER CONTROL

long time ago I tried online dating. One guy that I briefly emailed with (never met him in person), let's call him Cosimo, told me that in his quest to understand women, he had "paid a lot of PhDs, MDs and epidemiologists" until he had found a female "expert" whose advice worked for him.

Cosimo told me he had paid big bucks to attend a two-day seminar with her. "As a man, having a woman help me understand women from a man's view was a transformational information exchange," (huh?) he said. "In fact, I have applied a number of her suggestions about women's behavior and it has helped me dramatically."

Sounds wonderful, doesn't it? Wouldn't you commend a man for trying to understand women? Sure! But wait.

Cosimo kept going. I guess that to prove his expertise in women, he wrote:

> *Feelings are vital organs for a woman, not so much for men. We have them, but they don't drive us around—at least not the successful business guys running and managing major corporations in this country.*

Am I the only one who reads that our lack of emotional control disqualifies us to run corporations? Now you see why I never had the chance to ask Cosimo why he had needed to hire epidemiologists (who study diseases!) to understand women. Oh, wait, I just got it as I write this! He didn't hire epidemiologists to understand women, but to understand *his* disease, which is called *prejudice*! (That's meant to be a joke. The truth is that most people who are prejudiced are not aware they are.)

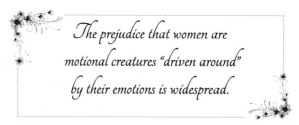

The prejudice that women are emotional creatures "driven around" by their emotions is widespread.

I've even heard people say this is why we shouldn't have a female president (regardless of her political party affiliation)! And what's truly a disgrace is that imposters are profiting from fueling prejudices and spreading discriminatory myths. Enough ranting. Let me control my emotion (anger), fix my hair, and move on. Done.

The fact is stereotypes negatively affect women's career advancement opportunities. They create discomfort and psychological distance, and get in the way of positive communication. That's why, before addressing what you (and every other *woman*) can do to manage emotions in a positive way, we'll dispel some myths that may be negatively affecting *you* and your professional development, if you have been led to believe they are true.

Truth or Myth? Men Make Rational Decisions and Women Decide on Emotions

Myth.

Both women *and* men decide on emotions. The only humans who don't are psychopaths. And yes, some of the people leading corporations are—indeed— psychopaths. Actually, there are four times as many psychopaths running major corporations as there are in society at large.[1]

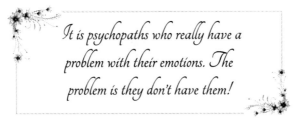

It is psychopaths who really have a problem with their emotions. The problem is they don't have them!

Psychopaths lack the tender feelings the rest of us take for granted. They lack the things that make you human: empathy, remorse, loving kindness.[2] Psychopaths turn into performers when they need to mimic normal human emotions they have never felt.[3] (No, we don't know whether your ex-boss was one of them, sorry.)

Such an abnormal percentage of CEOs being psychopaths is unsettling. Still, it's only 4%. This means, Cosimo, that 96% of the people that are running this country (overwhelmingly male) make decisions based on their emotions.[4] In other words, the people that "drive the world around" are "being driven around" by their emotions.

The best salespeople know and bank on that. (Moms know that too.) Consider for instance how people make their shopping decisions:

> When our emotional desires begin to shift toward a prospective brand, we align our reasons to be consistent with that intention. Our critical mind is always looking for evidence to support our beliefs. The stronger the emotion, the stronger the belief, and the greater the tendency is to seek out supporting evidence. We are not rational. We are rationalizers.[5]

It's like when you find a pair of Jimmy Choo® stilettos that you really, really like and you want to make it okay to charge $1,495 bucks to your VISA®. You start telling yourself how important it is to buy quality, how long they'll last, and that your professional image is key to be promoted. Aha.

I know that's how I shopped when I married my ex (I wish I had gone for the shoes.) Everyone who has retrospectively admitted that ignoring red flags leads to bad decisions can relate to the fact that we are not as smart, rational, or unbiased as we'd like to believe we are. The neuropsychological research and literature that supports this is not only extensive,[6] but fascinating.

You'll want to read more about this topic. It will improve your emotional intelligence.

How Knowing That Both Men and Women Decide on Emotions Will Benefit You

- Now you know what to reply when someone accuses you of being a woman, and therefore too emotional. (Just don't say it angrily.)
- Now you know why you shouldn't apologize for being emotional, so you won't. 99% of humans are. Which is great, by the way, because the 1% who are not (the psychopaths) may have excellent intellectual reasoning ability, but that's only in theoretical matters. When it comes to *real life* they show poor judgment and failure to learn by experience.[7]

Truth or Myth? You Can't Be Rational and Emotional at Once

Myth.

[While] emotions overwhelmingly drive behavior, it is misguided to believe that thinking and feeling are somehow mutually exclusive. Emotion and logic are intertwined.[8]

After conducting over 100,000 in-depth interviews of men and women executives in over 60 Fortune 500 companies, Barbara Annis and John Gray (yes, the author of *Men are from*

Mars and Women are from Venus) report that women deal with stress in a way that probably won't surprise you.

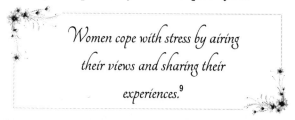

Women cope with stress by airing their views and sharing their experiences.[9]

This doesn't mean they're necessarily complaining or want an issue to be resolved immediately. Nor does it mean that women are less rational during an emotional moment and can't deal with the issue. Actually, women are oftentimes more capable than men are of experiencing strong emotions and thinking rationally at the same time.[10]

Don't you wish more people knew that? Here I go again with that Cosimo guy (grrrr). Look at what he also said he learned in that seminar about understanding women:

Women talking . . . Really, who would talk for an hour about a subject and not really want any help? So many women just want to share their experience and make me listen?????? What is a man supposed to do - - - - answer . . . shut up, listen, and ask "is there anything else honey"? As a man, if I am talking to a man about a problem, and he has a suggestion, I want to hear it, because I want my problem to go AWAY. I don't enjoy just fracking talking about it. (This lesson alone was worth the tuition!!!)

Other than "Wow, I had never seen anybody use that many question marks together!" let's extract some value from this comment: Men can be really confused when we don't behave like a man. I wish that speaker had explained to them that this female behavior in no way reduces our ability to think rationally, as Annis and Gray explained.

How Knowing That Emotion and Logic Are Intertwined Will Benefit You

- Understand how men may misinterpret your behavior, so during a difficult conversation (when you may be stressed) you'll increase your chances of being understood and respected if you are brief, concise, and try to keep the conversation on a rational level.

- Now you know why you'll be better off leaving the emotional explanations for some other time (or some other person).

Truth or Myth? Women Are More Emotional than Men

Myth.

And a big, fat one. So fat, that even women believe it! (I know I used to.) Men are every bit as emotional as women. Why do people believe that women are more emotional, then? In one study almost 100% of Americans 18-29 expressed that "emotionality is more true for women."[11] I don't know, but I can think of some possibilities:

- In studies of 23,000 from 26 countries, women more than men reported themselves open to feelings.[12]

- Men prefer not to show their emotions—unless they're pretty stressed, and then only to those close to them.[13] They conceal their emotions probably because most people associate being emotional with being weak.[14]

- When men show their emotions, they do it in a way that's different from women's.

- When a man is upset, for instance, he may display hostile or aggressive behaviors, whereas a woman may cry first and then express aggression with words.

- Most people are not aware that biological research does not support the theory of differences in emotions between men and women. Stereotypes that women are more emotional are based on at least three ideas: menstrual cycle mood swings, maternal instinct, and emotional expressivity. However, support for these stereotypes is weak.[15]

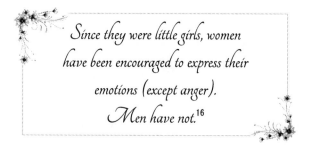

Since they were little girls, women have been encouraged to express their emotions (except anger).
Men have not.[16]

- Women have a more complex and differentiated vocabulary to describe emotional experiences, and this happens across different age groups and socioeconomic levels. For instance, if you asked people, "How would you feel if your best friend moved away to a better job?" a man could say "I'd feel bad," whereas a woman could say, "I'd feel bittersweet," or "I'd feel both happy and sad."[17]

- If a woman expresses an emotion such as anger, fear, sadness, or disgust, people think it's because she's emotional. If a man displays the same level and type of emotion, people think it's because "he's having a bad day." In an experiment researchers showed people photos of men and women expressing those four emotions (anger, fear, sadness, and disgust) and told them the circumstances the people in the photos were facing. For instance, for anger, "Got yelled at by the boss;" for fear, "Was chased by an angry bear;" for sadness, "Buried a family pet" and for disgust, "Took a large gulp of sour milk," and many others. Here's what they reported:

Despite being given situational information to explain the emotional behavior on every trial, both male and female participants were more likely to judge that women's emotional behavior was caused by their emotional nature, whereas men's behavior was caused by a situation that warrants it.[18]

It seems to me the findings from that experiment may be interpreted as, "He has a valid reason," and "She's hormonal." Am I being hormonal because I don't like being called hormonal?

How Knowing That Men Are as Emotional as Women Will Benefit You

- Even though a man may not express emotions as you would, that doesn't mean he's not feeling them. Don't assume he doesn't care.

- With the idea we've discussed of how mirroring the other person is a technique that works to lower defenses, mirroring a man's level of emotional expression may make him feel more comfortable entering in dialogue with you.

Truth or Myth? Your Culture Influences How You Deal with Emotions

Truth.

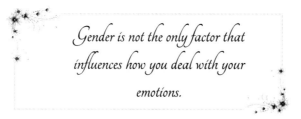

Gender is not the only factor that influences how you deal with your emotions.

Many factors determine how you deal with emotions, such as your culture ("the way we do things around here" you learned from the group you were part of when growing up) and your personality (which is made of your genetics and your experiences.)

When it comes to cultures other than their own, most people's knowledge is as limited as the tip of an iceberg. They know about the six Fs: food, fashion, festivals, folklore, famous people, and flags (and other symbols). But differences based on the six Fs are merely superficial.

The real differences among people of various cultures are way deeper and way bigger–like the full body of the iceberg. They go beyond whether they like tacos, sushi, or hot dogs, coffee, sake, or tea. It's not whether a woman wears a khaleeji dress or capris, or what date they associate with independence. And is certainly not accurately represented by Antonio Banderas for all Spaniards, by Gerard Depardieu for all French, or by Sofia Vergara for all Colombians.

Cultural differences involve differences in values and beliefs, in ways to discern what's right from what's wrong, in ideas about how we should treat others, etc.

With more people coming from other countries, or having been raised by immigrant parents or grandparents, developing cultural competency is becoming more and more important. One of the things that we learn at home is, for instance, whether showing our emotions openly is or is not acceptable behavior when we are upset at work.

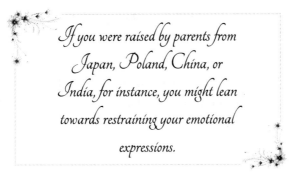

If you were raised by parents from Japan, Poland, China, or India, for instance, you might lean towards restraining your emotional expressions.

Affectively neutral cultures tend to keep their emotions controlled and subdued.

In contrast, if your parents came from Egypt, Cuba, Spain, Philippines, Russia, or Italy, which are cultures *high in affectivity*, chances are finding an immediate outlet for your emotions is completely acceptable to you. Even if your family was born in the U.S. for many generations, your ethnic group influences how you were socialized, as well as the stereotypes people may hold about you, for good or for bad.

How Knowing That Your Culture Influences How You Deal with Emotions Will Benefit You

- This is, as every other cultural generalization, not an absolute: there are always exceptions. Still, understanding that people are at different levels in the spectrum of visible "emoting" will help you understand (and adapt to) others better, especially those who are very different from you. For instance, studies show that black women, by virtue of their biculturalism in being members of two ethnic identity groups (the black group and the white group), cultivate sophisticated adaptive skills.[19]

- This ability to become "bicultural" (adapt to the other person's cultural style) will help you navigate difficult conversations better. It has also been proven to be a critical component of effective leadership.[20]

Emotional Control 101

When I feel passionate about a topic, I tend to express my views in a way so intense that people may think I'm upset. I'm almost never upset, but in my culture expressing emotions is the norm.

> *If you are like me, not showing your emotions is a big challenge, especially when they are intense.*

My point is that whether your emotions are positive or negative it's a good idea to keep them at bay because, as you read before, most people think that they override your rationality. If you feel that you really, really can't, then use your exit line. But it's not a good idea to overuse exit lines, so let's talk about how you can maintain control of your emotions while having the difficult conversation.

So, Can You Control Your Emotions?

Well, no. Not really. But it doesn't matter, because you can control what happens *before* and what happens *after* you have an emotion. What happens before an emotion is a *thought*. It is a thought you had, or a story you told yourself, that triggers a certain emotion.

> *By controlling your thoughts, emotions control themselves.*

You see? And, on top of that, you can control what happens *after* the emotion, which is your *conscious response* to it. This is how our emotions and our rational thinking are intertwined: emotions are the ham (or the zucchini if you're vegetarian) of your sandwich, and thoughts are the bread.

How Emotions Work

The diagram on the next page shows how emotions work. It looks a bit convoluted, right? But it's actually easy to understand. Go check it out before you read on. I'll wait here.

1. First, something happens (the trigger)

This is the event that triggers the emotion. For instance, it's 9:30 a.m. and your boyfriend, who was supposed to meet you for a very important meeting at 10:00, texts you that he will be 45 minutes late. "Oh no," you may be thinking, "I'd be very upset!" True, but not yet. Before that emotion pops up in step 4, two other things happen in nanoseconds (Yes, THAT fast).

2. You filter the event through your experience

Your values, belief system, similar events from your past, etc. have left a footprint on your life that permeates how you construct your reality. Your personality is also a factor in the mix. Let's say that your parents taught you punctuality as a value. Let's also say that your former boyfriend was always on time, and your current boyfriend is usually late. Let's also say that you're not a very patient person. All of these factors will influence how you interpret the event, which is the next step.

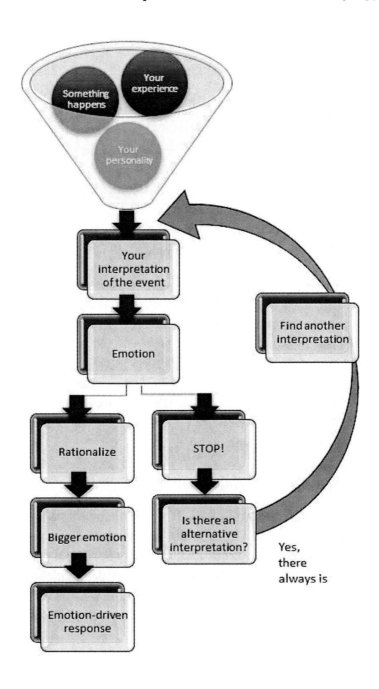

3. You interpret the event

In other words, you judge what happened, and in many cases you make it about you, even when that may not be the case. Oh, and this interpretation is something that you tell yourself. Because we are always chatting with ourselves, aren't we? You may tell yourself something like, "I should have told him it was at nine, not ten. I knew he would be late—I knew it! This just shows he doesn't care about me. He knew how important this meeting was for me!" And on and on. That interpretation is what triggers an emotion.

This interpretation is only one out of an infinite number of possible interpretations. It was your choice to pick this one.

4. Now the emotion pops up

The emotion arises, but not before the previous steps. My guess is that you're feeling upset at your boyfriend. Perhaps you want to cry. You may start to feel the physical signs of the emotion you're feeling.

This is where the road divides. Do like I do: when you come to a fork in the road, take it! You can react to the emotion in two possible ways: passively or actively.

5a. The passive reaction

This is what you do when you just let your emotions keep flowing like a river and you float on it. What will automatically happen is that your brain will start *rationalizing* the emotion, validating it.

This is what you're doing when the little voice inside of your head is telling you why you have every right to feel the way you do, and how *everyone* else would feel the same way ("If it was my brother-in-law who did this to my sister she would raise hell when he got here!")

This is also where the "shoulds" that you've developed in life pop up: "A gentleman should never have his girlfriend waiting so long!" By doing this you are actually *protecting* the emotion, so it grows like a fire you're throwing wood into.

It is at this stage when your fears can take over and tell you what to do. Their advice may be geared towards protecting you from threats that are not real, and this may hinder your openness to solving the problem in a way that benefits both parties. For instance, that internal voice may tell you something like, "The truth is that I'm *not* that upset—it's honestly not a big deal, *but* if I don't make a scene he will do it again." Do you see how this is a response motivated by fear, not by the desire to find a constructive solution to this problem?

Note: This reaction is only one out of an infinite number of possible reactions, and it was your choice to pick this one.

5b. You can react the active way

The active way is when you *consciously* tell yourself to stop and be rational.

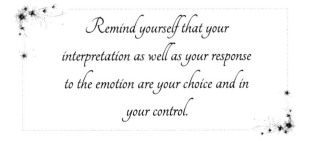

Remind yourself that your interpretation as well as your response to the emotion are your choice and in your control.

Breathe and interrupt the inertia that was taking you towards an emotion-driven response.

Then you go back to the beginning, and *reinterpret.* Is there an alternative interpretation? There always is. Could it be that your boyfriend had a car accident that wasn't even his fault? What if a puppy crossed in front of him, coming out of nowhere, and your boyfriend couldn't brake, but was decent enough to take the doggy to the vet, knowing you'd agree that he'd do that even if that meant being late? Could it be that his son, who has juvenile diabetes needed to be taken to the emergency room (again) this morning? It could be.

I'll say it again: you don't know what you don't know. Let me ask you, if you think of the puppy or of his son, do you still feel as upset towards your boyfriend? I bet you don't. I bet your emotion automatically changed when you changed your interpretation of the event.

Stop Making Everything Personal

Sometimes we make it about ourselves when it has nothing to do with us, isn't that true? It seems that sometimes we think we are more important than we are.

Research suggests that *Taking Conflict Personally* (TCP) is a trait,[21] just like being patient, jealous, ambitious, or optimistic, which would mean that some of us are more prone to TCP than others. TCP is not a fun trait. It is "the feeling of being personally engaged in a punishing life event," and it makes a person feel devalued, threatened, anxious, and insulted while engaging in conflict.[22]

Who would want to cultivate such a trait? Nobody. The same way you can turn yourself from a pessimist into an optimist by intentionally reprogramming your brain, you can decide to stop taking things personally.

Ponder your answers to the following questions in order to make a quick self-assessment of your level of TCP:[23]

- How much does it hurt your feelings to be criticized?
- Do you take it very personally when the rest of the group rejects one of your suggestions?
- Do you think that if you make a bad suggestion people will think you're stupid?
- Do stressful discussions make your stomach hurt?
- Do you think that conflict discussions can really jeopardize friendships?
- Do you really hate arguments?

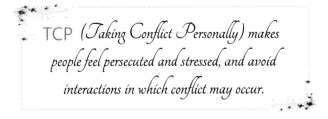

TCP *(Taking Conflict Personally) makes people feel persecuted and stressed, and avoid interactions in which conflict may occur.*

What's ironic though is that the same people who want to avoid conflicts, tend to become *unusually* aggressive once the argument starts.[24] Why would that be?

Two possible explanations have been offered.[25] One is that the person high in TCP feels so intensely punished and stressed by conflict, which she associates with aggression, that she overcompensates. She might intentionally adopt a special arguing persona modelled on aggressive stereotypes, as she may believe that people are supposed to be unusually competitive during arguments.

The second hypothesis is that an unusually aggressive person has become high in TCP because he has actually experienced an unusually high proportion of arguments which escalated out of control and were extremely punishing. What do you think? I've seen people who fit both possibilities. Do you think that any of them may apply to you?

TCP has many more negative side effects (besides stress), such as blurring our vision (how can you see things clearly if you're feeling hurt?) and hindering constructive dialogue that could lead to everyone-wins solutions (TCP makes you believe that for someone to win the other person has to lose, so you don't even see everyone-winning as an option.) Anything else? Oh, yeah: TCP is contagious![26]

We are hardwired to protect ourselves, but when we make a conscious effort to understand what's happening and then decide to reframe a situation, we can control our tendency to take things personally.

Did you see how in the previous scenario you were thinking that your boyfriend was late because he didn't care about you, and it ended up being about a puppy or his son?

Use a TATER™ To Manage Your Emotions

Do you like taters? They will help you remember the acronym I've created for the steps you'll need to follow next time you want to get a better grip on your emotions:

- **T** is for *triggers*. Step one is to anticipate triggers.
- **A** is for *attention*. Step two is to shift your attention.

- **T** is for *thoughts*. Step three is to change your thoughts and interpretations.
- **E** is for *expectations*. Step four is to adjust your expectations.
- **R** is for *response*. Your last step is to decide your response.

T Is for Triggers

Start by anticipating the circumstances that trigger unwanted emotions. If you can, avoid them.

For instance, when you talk to your sister on the phone and her kids are constantly interrupting it may make you feel frustrated. You can't change her circumstances but you can schedule a private time to talk face-to-face next time you need her undivided attention. (Did you notice that *undivided* is divided?)

If you know that you're more likely to get stressed when traffic is heavy, plan to leave your home 15 minutes earlier next time. If you know that your supervisor tends to make comments that you take personally and hurts your feelings, read about TCP before the meeting and prepare psychologically to detach yourself from those comments when they occur.

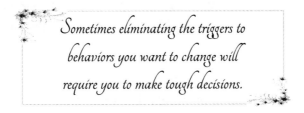

Sometimes eliminating the triggers to behaviors you want to change will require you to make tough decisions.

I used to smoke, and when I decided to quit, I stopped visiting one of my best friends because at her house everyone smoked. At first, I just claimed I was too busy to visit her, and this was true in a way. It was a very difficult decision to make because we loved each other and I missed spending time with her. That was before I dared to speak assertively. One day, I decided to tell her the real reason why I had stopped going, and you know what she said? "Oh! I won't smoke when you visit me! Spending time with you is more important than a stupid cigarrette!" I still avoid being around smokers though.

A Is for Attention

Imagine you are getting ready for a very important meeting (or date) and you notice you have a pimple on your nose. Or a spot on your blouse. Or 20 more pounds than a year ago. It happens. If you keep your attention on the pimple, spot, or love handles you will likely feel less confident and more anxious. Unwanted emotions. You need to make a conscious effort to focus your attention on the great quality of your presentation, or on your friendly personality.

A common source of dissatisfaction is our tendency to compare ourselves with others whom we consider better than us in a certain area. Like when you go to the gym for the first time and look at all the people with athletic bodies, and you make yourself miserable or guilty. Why not, instead, focus on the fact that you have started going to the gym? Or on other accomplishments?

T Is for Thoughts

Replace the thoughts or beliefs that lead you to the unwanted emotion with other thoughts or beliefs. The technical name is *cognitive reappraisal*.

Next time you feel an unwanted emotion, ask yourself "What thought did I have that lead me to feel this way?" and "What do I believe about the situation that is leading me to have those thoughts?" It's not easy, but when you think that it's all about the stories you tell yourself, you can start getting a grip on your emotions by telling yourself different stories.

> *Once you work on your interpretations and therefore reactions, you will see a huge change in your life.*

When you work on your interpretations your stress will go down. Like way down! Things in life that bothered you before won't bother you as much or at all. You will be able to control your emotions much more effectively and you will not ever want to go back to letting your emotions run you.

E Is for Expectations

Adjust your expectations. If they are unrealistic you will likely be disappointed, and that's not a good feeling. Perfectionism may also cause frustration and lower self-esteem, so have some self-compassion and reconsider if you're aiming too high. Think big, but don't set yourself up for failure.

I recognize sometimes I'm a bit of a perfectionist. What have I done about it? Well, I bought a magnet that reads "Life doesn't need to be perfect to be wonderful." I set it on my desk in front of me whenever I'm working (guess why). It does help! I've also enlisted my co-author to help me. Whenever I'm stuck she says "Glue." That's our code. One day she kept saying "Glue!

Glue! Glue!" and I had forgotten, so I just kept wondering why she was acting like a fish. I just ignored her. We just do that to each other sometimes. Later, when we compared notes, we cracked up.

Sometimes it's not your expectations that you need to adjust, but a specific situation. Let's say that in the past you've planned the *perfect* company event, but the speaker was not as entertaining as you thought he'd be, some guests were late, food was insipid, and chairs were uncomfortable. Well, next time you plan an event don't expect it to be perfect, and consider a different venue, different speaker, etc. That may reduce negative emotions before, during, and after that next event.

R Is for Response

The last step is controlling your response. This is the most difficult part and takes the most practice. Remember that you have a choice in how you respond. You actually get to make the decision. You have control over yourself. Many times we feel out of control but we don't have to be. Pause and think before you just react. Instead, take a deep breath, drink water, take some time and if needed use your exit line and leave.

What Did You Learn?

Take some time to process what you read. Write a few notes. What did you learn in this chapter that you will use in your next difficult conversation? How can you control your emotional triggers? What will you tell yourself next time you're taking something personally?

CHAPTER EIGHT

WHAT NOT TO DO *DURING* THE DIFFICULT CONVERSATION

Don't Be Wishy-Washy

Connie Dieken, an Emmy® Award-winning former TV news anchor says, "If you sound like a wimp you'll be treated like one."[1] So don't. Don't sound apologetic, don't hesitate, don't look to others for validation, and don't use qualifiers or weak words.

How will you know if you do? As a first step start paying attention to your word choice. Think before, during, and after you speak. Make it a point to become aware. It's a good idea to take notes. (We know you may not do it, but it still is a good idea.) As a second step, some of you will want to ask a friend to give you honest (and tough) feedback. Just don't pick a friend that's wishy-washy herself! Consider role-playing your upcoming difficult conversation with your friend. If you do so, give her the following list of behaviors you want to master.

- **Avoid using filler words** or expressions, such as "um," "uh," "like." Here is a hot tip on how not to use filler words. If you have one you are particularly used to saying, focus on that word. Even write it down on a piece of paper while you practice. When you focus on it, you are less likely to say it.

- **Avoid using qualifiers.** A qualifier is something you say before your question or sentence that makes it sound apologetic, or that discounts it. For instance, "I know this is a stupid question, but . . .", or "I haven't been in this job long enough, but . . ."

- **Avoid asking for validation.** Ending a question with "Don't you agree?" "Am I right?" "What do you think?" too many times, or in need of validation rather than to open up dialogue, makes you sound indecisive. Don't do it. Instead use a pause so the other person can insert his thoughts.

- **Avoid asking for permission if possible.** Instead of saying "Would it be okay if I . . .?" when you don't need the other person's permission to do something makes you sound too eager to please, and therefore weak. I know a girl that asks for permission for everything. For instance, she called a lost-and-found service looking for the pillow she left at the airport, and after they told her "No, nobody has brought a pillow yet," she said, "Oh. Would it be okay if I called again in a few days to see if you have it?" Of course they said yes, that's how it works! How about, instead say (in a pleasant tone): "Thanks. I'll call again in a few days," or just "Thanks."

- **Avoid over explaining.** While research shows that the word *because* is one of the most powerful words in the English language, you want to avoid over explaining. You don't want to behave like someone who makes excuses rather than someone who assumes responsibility. Telling people *why* is a powerful tool to gain compliance, so use it wisely.

- **Avoid using accusatory adjectives.** Being too aggressive is not a good idea. Avoid applying adjectives or negative statements to the other person ("You are lazy." "You are wrong." "You are irresponsible." etc.)

Actually, all of those recommendations are best practices that you can use in your daily life, not only when you're having difficult conversations. The more you polish your communication skills, the better negotiator you'll be.

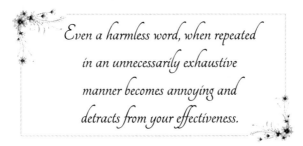

Even a harmless word, when repeated in an unnecessarily exhaustive manner becomes annoying and detracts from your effectiveness.

I remember a young woman I saw at an airport once during a business trip. She was the airline agent in charge of boarding. After she grabbed the microphone it didn't take more than a few minutes to see she could have benefited from a business communication class. She said something like, "Good afternoon *guys*.

We are about to board flight 1028 to Orlando. Thank you for your patience *guys*. We're running late, but we will keep you *guys* informed. Thank you *guys*."

With new phones and computers allowing you to record your script when rehearsing it, becoming a better communicator has become a lot easier.

At the end of this chapter you'll read about a few techniques you'll be able to use to change your wishy-washy behaviors.

Don't Ramble

Some people say women ramble. Sometimes it's true. But I don't think it's always true. I mean, what is always true? I guess a lot of things when you really think about it. Oh wait. Am I rambling?

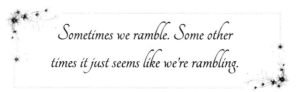

Sometimes we ramble. Some other times it just seems like we're rambling.

That's because many of us favor a communication style (circular and indirect) that's opposite from men's favored communication style (linear and direct), which is the rule in today's business world.

Linear vs. Circular Communication Styles

This is what the two styles looks like. Different, huh?

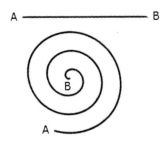

The linear style is conducted in a straight line, moving in a linear way from point A (the start of the conversation) to point B (the main point).

"Getting to the point" is very important and the point is stated explicitly.

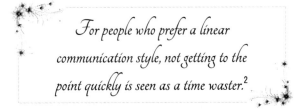

For people who prefer a linear communication style, not getting to the point quickly is seen as a time waster.[2]

Now contrast it with the circular style, in which the speaker gives all necessary contextual elements which listeners can connect to understand what she means.[3] In other words, the conversation starts in point A, but *before* getting to the main point (B), the speaker feels that she needs to give you the background (the spiral that gets closer to point B gradually), so you will understand the main point (B) better when (and if) she gets to it.

Here's an example of how this works. In my conferences on leadership I sometimes ask the audience, "Imagine that you are the parent of two kids, one who is great at math and the other who is great at basketball. Summer is approaching and you want to send each of them to a camp. You can send each kid to just one camp, and you've found two camps close by you can afford. You guessed it, a math camp and a basketball camp. Which camp do you send each kid to (they can both go to the same or each of them to a different one)?"

Sometimes, before each team has the chance to share their answer with the group, someone asks me, "Why wouldn't someone choose the camp their kid likes the most?" and my answer is, "I can see why you think that: that's in line with mainstream American culture's way of thinking. Wait until the other teams share their answers and you might be surprised.

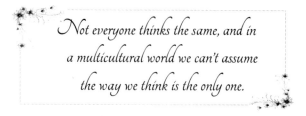

Not everyone thinks the same, and in a multicultural world we can't assume the way we think is the only one.

People think in ways that you couldn't even imagine!

Then I ask each team to share their thoughts. I get all kinds of answers: some teams would send both kids to math camp, arguing that math is an important skill for life and that kids can play basketball at home. Some others say just the opposite: the kids have worked enough on academics during the school year, and summer is for being outdoors and having fun. A third answer I hear all the time is that they'd send each kid to their non-favorite theme camp, because they see value in raising balanced kids. (Child rearing practices vary widely by culture. Some Chinese-American mothers, for instance, believe that kids don't like something because they're not good at it, but once they've practiced enough to be good they will like it.)

I use this exercise to open up the discussion about leaders building on people's strengths, but that's another story. Do you see how I'm writing in a circular manner? Good insight! Well, the point is (now I switched to linear) that men tend to give me answers like, "I'd send each kid to whatever they like most." And they shut up. Done. And only if I ask, "Why?" they explain.

Not always, but quite frequently, women give me answers like, "Interesting you asked, because I actually had to make a similar decision a few years ago . . ." and they go on to tell me the story. I sometimes interrupt them and ask, directly, "But which camp would you send each kid to?" and the answers I get range from, "Hold on, that's where I'm going" to a nod (while they keep going with the story).

I don't have a scientific explanation, but my guess is that it's our empathy that—again—is working against us. It's as if we wanted to pave the way, and we feel that we're making it easier for the other person to understand our point. Well, we're not. We may actually be making it more confusing for the listener. He or she may get distracted thinking "Where is she going with this?" "Why is she telling me this?" People don't know what specifically to pay more attention to when listening. Or, they may just tune you out.

Direct vs. Indirect Communication Styles

Direct communicators are not ambiguous. Their message does not depend on the context—it is fully contained in their words.

> *Direct communicators "say it like it is." Indirect communicators hint.*

Indirect communicators hint, suggest, modulate their voice to change the meaning, or imply, and it's up to the receiver to "read between the lines."

The context is very important, because it's part of the message. Some indirect people may even say to person number one a statement intended for person number two (who is within earshot). In indirect communication it is also possible that messages will be sent through a third-party intermediary.

It is actually very interesting how different cultures (or ethnic groups) favor different styles. For instance, in group-oriented cultures, like most Latin American and most Asian cultures, where the well-being of the community is placed above the well-being of its individual members, people tend to use an indirect style. This style is used in order to let others save face, to avoid confrontations, or to preserve harmony.

In Japan, for instance, being good at "reading the air" is an important communication skill. Reading the air means decoding body language, considering the context, and understanding hints. Since women tend to be more relational than men, it comes as no surprise their style is closer to the *indirect* side in the communication continuum.

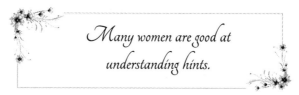

Many women are good at understanding hints.

Here's an example. I was conducting an intercultural communication competency workshop for a client in California. This is a state agency that's incredibly multicultural: in my group of 20 people I had representatives from the U.S., Egypt, Pakistan,

Korea, Taiwan, Mexico, Russia, and China. Talk about a diverse group!

I asked for a volunteer from the U.S. and one from any other place. A Chinese woman (let's call her Magnolia) and an American man (let's call him Zane) jumped up. Perfect. So I explained to both of them, "You know that I flew from Kansas City to Los Angeles for this workshop, right?" They both nodded. "Now imagine at 4:00 p.m., when the class is over, it's only you and me in here, and I ask you, "Do you know how much a taxi would charge me for a ride to the airport? I'm flying home tonight and I don't have a rental car. I'm worried it may be too expensive."

A couple of people in the audience smiled, like a Mexican guy, in a way that seemed they knew where I was going. (Being Mexican he was used to indirect communication, so he had already *decoded* my *hint*.)

Then I looked at Zane and said, "What would you say?"

"I have no idea, because I don't take taxis. But maybe when you call the taxi company they can give you an estimate," he replied. Direct, concise, solution oriented. Great.

Then I looked at Magnolia. "What would you say?"

"I would ask you if you want me to give you a ride," she said. She had decoded my indirect message nicely!

"Unbelievable!" exclaimed Zane (and you should have seen his body language, as direct as him!) "If that's what you wanted then why didn't you just say so?"

As a direct communicator he expected the same from me. No style is better than the other, but when you're having a difficult conversation, it is a great idea to be open to the possibility that the other person is using a style different than yours and adapt accordingly.

> *The Golden Rule of treating others like you want to be treated doesn't always work in a multicultural environment.*

And I'm not talking about specific workplaces like the one I described, I'm talking about every workplace, because all of them have people from different nationalities, different races and ethnicities, different age groups, different personality styles, different regions of the country, and different genders.

No woman I've ever asked has doubted that men are a different culture. And the same is true for men.

Remember that "deep down we're all the same" is a fallacy, and when it comes to communicating with people from a different culture, it is a fallacy that can cause a lot of trouble.

> *People who study intercultural communication abide by the Platinum Rule: treat others the way they want to be treated.*

It's *How* You Speak

It's not *how much* you talk—it's *how* you talk. While linear or direct communicators may be seen as blunt, rude, aggressive, unfeeling and blind to the impact of their words on others, circular communicators often appear disorganized, slow witted, and unable to track the point of the discussion, at least to more direct speakers; indirect communicators may not even be understood.

None of those characterizations need be accurate,[4] but they may affect your credibility or reduce the impact of your requests.

I am going to recommend that you start practicing identifying these styles in other people first and then on yourself. Make it a point to analyze the speech pattern of one or two people a day.

Being linear or circular is not black or white—it's a continuum where some people are closer to one extreme than to the other. Start noticing where people fall and that will allow you to catch yourself when you seem to be rambling.

Explain only if it's necessary when talking to a linear/direct communicator. Learn that you don't always need people's approval or agreement.

> *When speaking with a linear/direct communicator, be direct, concise, and say your most important message first.*

And when speaking with a circular/indirect person be patient, ask questions to make sure you're understanding, use the echo technique to confirm you've decoded the message appropriately, and try to "tone down" your own directness as to not seem too blunt.

Don't Be Overly Apologetic

There is ample evidence that women are more inclined to offer expressions of contrition than men.[5] (But you didn't need research to tell you that, right?)

While some researchers and authors seem to believe that women apologize too much, others argue that in truth, men apologize too little.[6] In my opinion both sides have merit.

What's important for you to know are the explanations they offer: men consider apologizing as a sign of weakness, and they refuse to apologize because they have difficulty admitting they are wrong.[7] Women readily apologize because they are more concerned than men with showing courtesy to other people.[8] Once again, I agree with all of them. As with any other generalization, this one should be taken for what it is, knowing that for every rule there's an exception.

What I've seen time and again is that in many cases women tend to say I'm sorry not to apologize, but to show empathy.

A co-worker says:	"I lost my cell phone."
You reply:	"Oh, I'm sorry."
A man replies:	"Where have you looked?"

Your boss says:	"I'm coming down with something."
You reply:	"Oh, I'm so sorry."
A man replies:	"Go home. I don't want to get sick!"

The problem is that under certain circumstances an "I'm sorry" may be taken as an admission of guilt.

Your boss says:	"What happened with the new client?

You reply: "They called this morning and
                     withdrew their order. I'm sorry."

Your boss is wondering what you did that caused them to cancel their order. Over apologizing may also make you look weak, so start improving your vocabulary and communication skills.

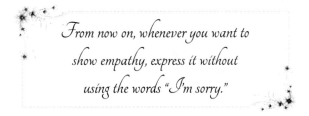

From now on, whenever you want to show empathy, express it without using the words "I'm sorry."

For example, "It's awful you had to go through that." Or "That must have been difficult." Now it's your turn, be creative!

And what if you really did make a mistake? In that case say "I apologize." And immediately add a sentence explaining what you will do to make sure it won't happen again:

> I apologize for coming in late this morning. From now on I will leave home 15 minutes earlier to ensure it won't happen again.

It sounds quite different than "I'm sorry," doesn't it? It doesn't sound aggressive, but solution-oriented. And, it certainly doesn't sound weak!

It's really important that you apologize appropriately. Apologies matter. They reduce anger and aggression and promote forgiveness and relationship well-being.[9] Without being overly apologetic, show how considerate and humble you are by offering apologies, and show your self-esteem by requesting them when appropriate. Apologize when you have offended the other person.

Don't Interrupt and Don't Let Them Interrupt You

Not interrupting is a challenge, for me, I admit. I tend to get very excited and feel like I can't wait to make my point. This goes along with listening. If you are a person that interrupts, slow down—you will get your turn.

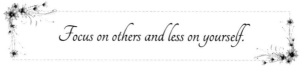

Focus on others and less on yourself.

But, how do you get someone to stop interrupting you? As with most bad behaviors, people will not stop unless someone points it out to them. However, if you do it the wrong way you can come across as rude and the other person might just shut down.

Let me tell you a story I read in the *New York Times* that is funny but it really is not funny. Google® Executive Chairman Eric Schmidt was invited to be a panelist at a conference in Austin, Texas, about—read this carefully, please—*gender and diversity issues*. This obviously was his chance to score some goodwill for Google by being empathetic and nice, right? Well, here's what he did: he *repeatedly* interrupted Chief Technology Officer Megan Smith, *the only woman* panelist on stage.

Oh, but it gets even better (or worse, actually!) Google®'s global diversity manager, who is *a woman* (Judith Williams) and was in the audience, *raised her hand* and asked Schmidt an uncomfortable question: "Given that unconscious bias research tells us that women are interrupted a lot more than men, I'm wondering if you are aware that you have interrupted Megan many more times [than the men]." Bam! Everyone applauded and articles about this started popping up online, with titles like, "Don't interrupt when a woman is talking about corporate diversity" (*TIME*®), "Google® executive Eric Schmidt, man, makes total ass of himself at SXSW" (*The Verge*®), or "Equal parts hilarious and depressing" (*Salon*®).

It frankly is depressing, and even more so because *both* men and women interrupt women almost *three times* as much as they interrupt men.[10]

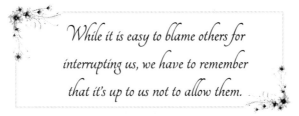

While it is easy to blame others for interrupting us, we have to remember that it's up to us not to allow them.

Here are a few ideas to deal with people who interrupt you. They vary in their level of intensity and "niceness," so pick the best one depending on your own style, the circumstances, and with a quick assessment of the other person's intentions:

- When the person interrupts say, "I know you have good points too. Let me say what I need to say and then I promise I will listen to you." Then when the person interrupts again, say the same thing the same way. Make sure your voice tone stays as nice as it was the first time you said it. Be careful not to add in a hint of sarcasm.

- Say "Please let me finish," and keep talking.

- Another idea that works is to be silent when the person interrupts you. Then listen until she is finished, and even pause for a few seconds before speaking. Then begin by saying, "I appreciate what you've said, and now give me a couple of minutes to make my point." You may need to repeat this statement when she interrupts again.

- Get a whistle and everytime the other person interrups you blow it really loud. (Okay, maybe this one is a bit extreme.)

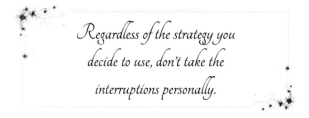

Regardless of the strategy you decide to use, don't take the interruptions personally.

People that interrupt usually interrupt everyone, so it's not personal. After the conversation, go back to your office, and start preparing a script similar to this one:

(F) Facts: <Interrupter's name>, earlier today when we were negotiating in your office, you interrupted me many times to reply before I had finished expressing my request. Like when <insert specific instance here>. If this was the first time I wouldn't bother having this discussion, but it is a pattern.

(E) Effect: When that happens we both waste time because neither of us understands the other.

(A) Acknowledge: I know you have great ideas and I want to hear them.

(R) Request: And that's why I came to ask you to please let me finish my sentences before you jump in. I'll make sure to reciprocate the courtesy.

> *If you notice that people (in general) tend to interrupt you quite frequently, look at yourself in the mirror.*

Ask yourself if it's possible that you ramble too much, or tend to keep the microphone too long, and then think of a better way to balance the dialogue.

I've seen that many women who keep the microphone too long know they do it—they just forget about it when they get on a roll. Others are not aware of what they do. Awareness is super important. Ask yourself, do I let others talk? Do I speak for a full five minutes before the other person can get a word in edgewise? If you've answered yes then STOP IT! If you talk that much I guarantee you people have stopped listening. Comedian Rodney Dangerfield once said, "I haven't spoken to my wife in years. I didn't want to interrupt her." So if you want people to talk to you (and to like you!), share the microphone.

Perhaps you don't talk to much, but you still get interrupted a lot. Could it be that you've been letting people step on you for too long and now you'll need to make an extra effort to start getting the respect that you need?

Perhaps you'll want to ask a good friend if any of those scenarios apply to you. Explain you're working on improving your communication skills, and tell her you have your helmet on, so she won't feel uncomfortable giving you an honest critique.

Don't Be Defensive

While we are talking about bringing down the other person's defenses, we need to remember to not be defensive ourselves.

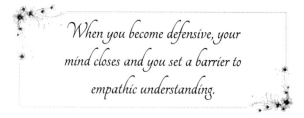

When you become defensive, your mind closes and you set a barrier to empathic understanding.

Your ego is more focused on protecting you from a perceived threat than on finding a solution to your problem. Your judgment gets blurred, and you may lose focus. Even worse, you become vulnerable to manipulation, because you have let the other person take control, and you may be willing to settle just to get the validation you need to feel better.

If you go into the conversation with any kind of a negative attitude, she will be defensive. If you want her to be less defensive, you have to be less defensive.

There was this guy Dax who, whenever something went wrong, managed to turn the tables and blame it on me. He was really good at doing it, I must admit. My reaction when he did that was to start explaining my side of the story, which really was a way of defending myself. Our conversations never ended well—we never found a solutions to any problem together. One day I decided to read again *The Seven Habits of Highly Effective People* book, the classic by Steven Covey. I remembered it addressed this issue.

After reading again about the habit of seeking first to understand and then to be understood, I decided to put it to the test next time I spoke with Dax. What I did was this: whenever I felt attacked, I just breathed, reminded myself of what I was doing (and *why* I was doing it), and asked him to clarify what he had said, instead of defending myself or trying to explain my side. It worked miraculously! After a while he stopped ranting, calmed down, and just said, "Thank you for listening." Then we went on with a respectful and collaborative conversation.

Dr. Fred Kofman, professor of leadership at *Universidad Francisco Marroquín* University in Argentina has an interesting technique you can learn and use to react less defensively. He explains that when the other person says, for instance, "You're wrong!" instead of reacting defensively ("Oh, yeah? Well, you are wrong—*more!*") you can reply, "What do you see that I don't?" Really listen to their reply, and only then, after you've heard and understood their side of the story you ask, "Now may I show you what I see that you haven't seen?"[11] Love it!

Don't Oversell

This section could have been added in the previous chapter as "Learn when to shut up!" Once the other person agrees with you, move to the conclusion to confirm the agreement, and leave.

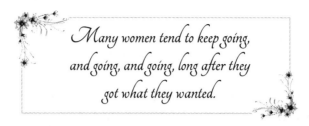

Many women tend to keep going, and going, and going, long after they got what they wanted.

My guess is that sometimes our excessive talking is our empathy acting against us. We want to make sure the other person is *happy* about the decision they just made, so we keep going hoping to make her feel better about it.

In my workshops for women, when I tell them that women don't know when to shut up they all crack up—and start talking about it, go figure. Picture this.

Ron goes to talk to his boss:

Ron: Knock, knock.

Boss: "Yes?"

Ron: "Donna, I need to leave early on Friday at 2.
            Is that okay?"

Boss: "That's fine."

Ron: "Thanks." Turns around and leaves.

Now picture Birdie.

Birdie: Knock, knock.
Boss: "Yes?"
Birdie: "Donna, I need to leave early on Friday at 2.
            Is that okay?"
Boss: "Fine."
Birdie: "Thank you so much! I wouldn't ask you un-
            less I really, really needed to leave. You see,
            the thing is that it's usually my husband who

> picks the kids up on Fridays to take them to the soccer game, but his company is having a sales event this weekend . . . Anyway, I'm talking too much, hahaha, I just want you to know that if I need to catch up with the ABC project, I'll come on Saturday . . ."

The funny thing is that when I act this out, everyone (men and women, yes, that's everyone) nods like, "Yeah, that's exactly how it is."

I'm sure there is more to say on the subject but let's follow our own advice. Let's stop talking about this and move on to some ideas on changing ourselves.

Change Those Bad Habits!

Okay, so you decided to become aware of the words you use, and possibly team up with a friend and have her observe you for a week. What you discovered is that, for instance, you say "I'm sorry" too much, or that you use filler words, or that you ramble when you're under stress.

Now what? Well, now you start working on changing. Here are a few techniques you can use to get rid of weak behaviors or poor communication habits such as the ones described in this chapter.

Rubber Band

Wear a rubber band like a bracelet. Every time you catch yourself doing the behavior you want to eliminate, pull it softly and let it hit you. Soft. It's not about hurting yourself, but about bringing awareness and punishing you a little so you won't do it again.

Bribe Yourself

Bribe yourself or reward yourself for small accomplishments. You can break a big goal into smaller ones and reward yourself along the way. When I was working on my doctorate I was often overwhelmed with the mere size of the project, so I found ways to treat myself with each difficult section I finished. The treat could be extra time with a friend or just a break. I couldn't have the treat until I finished my smaller goal.

Money Jar

Team up with someone and work together on eliminating each one's wishy-washy expressions. I met a couple of women in one of my workshops that told me they had a jar in their office, and whenever one of them used filler words, the other one extended her hand to get a dollar bill that she would drop in the jar. They were planning to go have fun and spend together what they had accumulated after a month of doing this.

Destroy Money

This technique is only for our international readers, because in the U.S. destroying money is illegal.

Pain is a stronger motivator than pleasure. Nothing wrong with the previous methods, but this one I'm about to tell you may work faster. First, pledge an amount, say twenty dollars, to eliminate *any* bad habit (oh yes, you can use this to quit smoking or to stop eating junk food too). How much is being a polished communicator worth to you? Twenty bucks? Fifty? Up to you. Let's say you pick 20 dollars. Break them into one dollar bills and give them to your friend. Every time she sees you doing the behavior you want to eliminate, she will tear a dollar bill in front of you. Yes, you read it right: destroy it! It is a horrible, sick thought, isn't it? I know! That's what makes this work.

If you knew that she was keeping the money or giving it to charity, you might think, "Mh. It's okay. No biggy." It would still make you feel good about yourself. But what if the money is destroyed forever, when there are so many people that could use it (including yourself)? Disgusting. You hate the waste so much that the mere thought of it makes you do whatever it takes to prevent you from seeing such a wasteful act again.

Have the Bad Guys Help You

If you thought that destroying money was horrible, I have something even worse. No kidding. Would you feel motivated to fulfill your commitment if you knew that if you don't *your* money will go to a cause that you are *against*? That's what stickk.com does with your hard earned beloved dollars if you fail!

Here's how it works. You sign a commitment contract (for instance "In four weeks I will not interrupt people at all.") You pledge a certain amount (say five dollars a week), and you pick an anti-charity that will get your money every week you fail to work towards your goal or fulfil your commitment.

An anticharity, for heaven's sake! Had you heard that term before? It refers to an orgnization you HATE. Incredible!

This crazy website was designed by two Yale professors who, for years, have conducted rigorous scientific research on how to help people stick to their goals.[12] What these scientists found is that the two factors that make people stick to their goals are incentives and accountability. And what better incentive than to keep your money away from the bad guys?

They have compiled a list of organizations on either side of several highly controversial issues, for instance *Americans United for Life* and *NARAL Pro-Choice America Foundation*, or pro-gun control and anti-gun control groups.

Passion is a strong motivator. The founders of stickk say their method triples the chances of people sticking to their goals, and I can see that. Can you? I'd rather get up two hours earlier to do what I've been procrastinating than see my money go to an organization called *Child Marriage Advocates*.

You feel me? If so, pick your method and just do it!

What Did You Learn?

Take some time to process what you read. Write a few notes. What did you learn in this chapter that you will use in your next difficult conversation? What communication style do you tend to use? How about the other people that tend to rub you the wrong way? Do you tend to interrupt people? What will you do about it? How will you stop interrupters? Are you too defensive? How will you change bad habits?

CHAPTER NINE

WHAT TO DO *AFTER* THE DIFFICULT CONVERSATION

Go Back to Normal

*T*he conversation is over. Now what? Sometimes it is simple and requires nothing but you walking away. Sometimes it requires a follow-up meeting and you need to set that before you leave.

> *Typically, the best thing to do is continue the relationship on the same level as before.*

Becoming suddenly super friendly or ignoring the person would not be good strategies. The key is to do things you would normally do with or around that person as soon as possible. Studies show that, on average, females are more forgiving than males,[1] so you want to make it obvious that you are moving forward and are fine with this person. Even if "fine" means, "we can maintain a working relationship." C'mon, not every work place needs to be Disneyland! (Although some may remind you of Disneyland's Haunted Mansion.)

What If They Don't Change?

But what if the person doesn't do what he said he would do? What if there is no change at all even though you agreed? As with most things, it depends. If you are a supervisor, then you need to document it (I actually suggest this for everyone) and use HR if you aren't sure of the protocol where you work.

But what if you aren't in a supervisory role? What if this is a spouse or friend? First, you know that you can't really change other people, as we discussed before; they have to be willing and able to change. Doing what I suggested can actually help you to be more persuasive but you can't make people change. Even a supervisor has limited means to insist on change. At most, this person can be fired but he still doesn't HAVE to change.

For instance, take my friend Marie, who wanted her husband to be less controlling and more affectionate. She was married to a dominating man for many years. All she wanted was to feel loved by him. He never told her she was pretty and his only compliment through the years was "You look nice." She clung to anything he did that could be interpreted as loving. He seemed to be embarrassed by her looks and would not bring her to his work events until a client of his said, "Your wife has a great personality! She is your best asset. You should let her come to these."

Marie's husband would call her in the middle of the day and say, "I see you went to Dunkin' Donuts. What did you buy? It looks like you bought a lot." Or "You went out to eat today. Who were you with?" Although she asked numerous times, he would not show her their finances.

Marie is a very affectionate person and he was not. He would hold her hand, only if she grabbed his but then would let go after less than a minute. Even their children noticed. "Daddy doesn't hug you but you hug him."

Despite all of this and more she was very committed to the marriage for personal reasons so she didn't plan on ever leaving him. She decided to make the best of living with someone like him.

It's not that she didn't ever speak up but she knew that if he considered it something uncomfortable or difficult, he would shut down. Therefore, she learned to mostly just do what it took to get along. She stifled who she was and stopped trying to have difficult conversations with him because he wouldn't listen, care, or change.

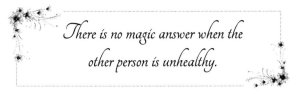

There is no magic answer when the other person is unhealthy.

Marie's husband is an example of someone who will not respond no matter how many good techniques and ideas you learn. If you are in this type of situation with a boss, co-worker or even your spouse, you have to decide how you will handle your situation. I wish I had some great answer for you like, "All you need to do is this one thing and then you'll get respect" but it's just not true.

You May Need to Use a New NO FEAR™

What are your choices with someone who is relatively healthy but hasn't changed? What I normally do is to just go back to the person and remind her about the conversation we had. You know the squeaky wheel gets the grease?

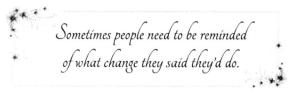

Sometimes people need to be reminded of what change they said they'd do.

You can even use the FEAR part of the NO FEAR™ method for that! Here's an example:

(F) Facts:

Ambrosia, remember last Friday when I asked you to start giving me your daily report by 11 a.m. the following day? You agreed you would begin doing that immediately.

Well, yesterday you turned in your daily report at 3 p.m., and on Tuesday you turned it in at 2 p.m.

(E) Effect:

I feel disappointed.

(A) Acknowledge: We had such a great conversation about it, and you were so understanding and positive!

(R) Request: So I now want to ask you to honor the commitment you made to me last Friday, starting tomorrow.

As you can infer from that script, last Friday my difficult conversation with Ambrosia was about her reports. Now it is about her lack of follow through. That makes them two different conversations so I don't sound like a broken record. That's why we should have ended the conversation on Friday with a verbal commitment on her part and a deadline, so that if needed I could call her on it.

Sometimes people won't change and you have no recourse. You can speak to him over and over but he won't change. If your request was reasonable, you made an effort, and were able to reach constructive dialogue this will be rare, so don't stress too much about it. But if the other person doesn't change you have to decide how far you will take it or if you are going to ignore their unwanted behavior.

I have a friend (we'll call her Alexa), whose husband liked to take his employees to lunch individually and as a group. When she realized that he was probably involved (still not real proof at that point) with an employee she asked him to stop having private lunches with the other woman. He absolutely refused. "I will not stop doing that, I also have private lunches with the other employees and it would be weird if I only stopped it with her."

Alexa had the difficult conversations over and over but he would not budge. Now, she had choices to make. Here are a few that she could have chosen:

- She could have screamed and shouted and went to his office and followed them to lunch and made a scene.

- She could have gone out on lunches with attractive men herself (an eye for an eye).

- She could have refused to speak to him until he stopped.

- She could have let him know she was upset about their lunches and otherwise maintain the marriage as usual.

Alexa chose the latter. He ended up leaving her anyway so we'll never know whether it would have mattered what she chose except he could claim she was a raving lunatic if she had chosen to scream!

The point is that no matter how many tactics she used, Alexa could not persuade him. He refused to stop having lunch (or an affair) with the other woman.

Some of you may be thinking that stopping the lunches with the other woman would have been like taking medication to cure the symptoms of a disease rather than the disease itself. Even if that was the case, though, Alexa's husband was not willing or able to collaborate with her. He chose lying over working together on improving their marriage, and cheating over being loyal to his vows, and that was his choice.

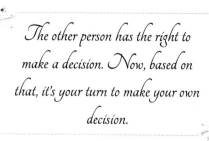

The other person has the right to make a decision. Now, based on that, it's your turn to make your own decision.

I won't go into the whole situation now, but what Alexa told me is that with the circumstances, she felt she had to find a way to go on and live with him even though she couldn't change this behavior.

Alexa assessed her options and made her choice. And that's what you need to do too.

Liked Best and Next Time (LB & NT)

You'll do your best to prepare, rehearse, and know what to do to leave the conversation victorious. That's great! However, it is possible that things didn't go exactly as you would have wanted them to go.

For instance, when you look back, you may realize that your level of confidence was not as it should have been, and this had a direct impact on a difficult conversation.

Many times it is a good idea to replay the conversations (or parts of it) in your head, just to figure out and name what you learned and what you did well. This will create neural networks that store the information in your brain in a way that are more readily available next time you're in a similar situation.[2]

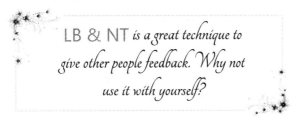

LB & NT *is a great technique to give other people feedback. Why not use it with yourself?*

The name is self–explanatory, so I know I'm risking sounding condescending here. Oh well, here I go: you tell yourself what did you like the best about *your* performance (throw yourself a bone!) and you also tell yourself what you plan on doing differently next time.

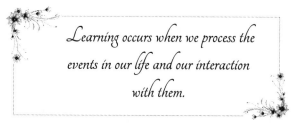

Learning occurs when we process the events in our life and our interaction with them.

Unless we reflect and make a decision for the future based on happenings, then we're just getting older but we're not gaining any experience. (WikiWomen, by the way, we don't get older. We just grow wiser.)

Let me give you an example of how I've used LB & NT to be better prepared in the future. A couple of months ago I knew that a person I was having a very difficult time with was coming to my house. I really didn't want to go home because I knew this was not going to be pleasant. But, I had to go home and I had to go home at that time. When I was a few blocks away, I felt my body tense up and my shoulders rise up. My stomach turned into knots as I slowly drove up. This is when I should have just gone inside my house without engaging the other person. But, I didn't and when the other person yelled at me I was sarcastic (my defense mechanism).

Afterwards, I've applied the LB & NT technique, and I've thought about how I mishandled the situation and how I should have listened to my body and calmed down before (if ever) engaging. On the other side, I also recognized what I did well: even though I wanted to, I didn't yell back.

This experience will help me remember to pay attention to my body. It has already helped me in other dealings with this person and even on a much smaller scale, with other people. In the future I will be able to say, "What I liked best is that I didn't overreact because I listened to my body!"

Don't Beat Yourself Up!

Replay the conversation only if you can keep it positive, constructive, and self-loving. Research shows that, while men tend to display behaviors that are *active-destructive* (effortful responses such as retaliating, expressing anger, or demeaning others), women are more prone to engaging in *passive destructive* behaviors, which are non-helpful responses that require little overt effort. Self-criticizing is one of them.

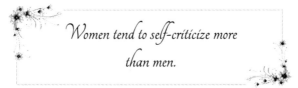

Women tend to self-criticize more than men.

Self-criticizing is defined as replaying the incident over in one's mind and criticizing one's self for not handling it better.[3] You wouldn't do that to your best friend, so don't do it to yourself. Be your own best friend.

Remember my friend Alexa, the one with the lunching/ cheating husband? (C'mon, it wasn't that long ago you met her.) Yes, that one. I saw her recently and she told me, "I have replayed the conversations enough that I learned and then I had to let them go." I commended her for that. Letting go is not easy, but she did it.

What an accomplishment, considering that women are more prone than men to experience increased emotional distress following a major trauma or life crisis, which leaves them more vulnerable to anxiety disorders.[4] Go Alexa!

Whenever you win you learn too, sure, but that motto is my way of acknowledging that even when things don't go my way there's still something good: there's a lesson for me to learn. I encourage you to share my motto and think of the positive things that usually come out of the negative ones, and most importantly, never (*never!*) let any event or person turn you against yourself. Never beat yourself up because of someone else's behavior, or because you were not perfect.

Nobody is. (Well, maybe except for Matt Damon.)

What Did You Learn?

Take some time to process what you read. Write a few notes. What did you learn in this chapter that you will use in your next difficult conversation? How will you manage to remain pleasant towards the other person if things don't go your way? What is your LB & NT from your last conversation?

ONE LAST WORD

*Y*ou can go into difficult conversations with your head held high.

We want to encourage you. You can do this.

You have the right to stand up for yourself. You have the right to a more positive environment and to be respected. You have the right to make the world a better place. You are a *Wiki-Woman*!

Keep this book handy because you will want to revisit this information. In order to fully digest and internalize what you have read, practice different areas in easier conversations. Think big, but start small—it only gets easier. Perhaps write down *NO FEAR*™ and keep it on your car visor or bathroom mirror.

Before we say "Til we meet again," we have a request for you (we are walking the talk and practicing our asking skills, as we've encouraged you to do.) If you enjoyed this book, act like a true wiki and help another woman by gifting a copy to her so she can benefit from what you learned.

Remember you are an agent of change. Over and over we find proof that when women collaborate with one another, they all benefit. We can attest to that firsthand. Take the initiative and partner up with another woman. You may have many friends, but what we're talking about here is not friendship—we're encouraging you to create a verbal contract with at least another woman, and committing to helping one another advance your careers. In general, women tend to seek mentors, but men get sponsors. Huge difference! We want to encourage you to sponsor another woman, and to find a sponsor for yourself.

We have nothing against men. We actually really (really!) appreciate them (one of us especially appreciates Matt Damon), but we know that women still face more challenges than men in the workplace. The challenges range from the gender wage gap to all kinds of bias that depart from traditional discrimination models, such as this one: when a woman teams up with men, it is the men who reap the rewards for the project's success, not the woman.[1] Interestingly enough, the same research that has arrived to the above conclusion, has found that when women team up with other women *everyone contributes and everyone benefits.*

Only joining forces we'll change that, so keep the energy flowing and our mission alive. Wiki on!

Sofia & Susan

Visit us at TheWikiWomenAcademy.com

REFERENCES

Introduction

1. Snyder, K. (2014). How to Get Ahead as a Woman in Tech: Interrupt Men. Retrieved on 2/14/2016 from http://www.slate.com/ blogs/lexicon_valley/2014/07/23/study_men_interrupt_women_ more_in_tech_workplaces_but_high_ranking_women.html.

2. Catalyst (2005). Women "Take Care," Men "Take Charge:" Stereotyping of U.S. Business Leaders Exposed. NY: Catalyst.

3. Catalyst (2007). The Double-Bind Dilemma for Women in Leadership: Damned if You Do, Doomed if You Don't. NY: Catalyst.

4. Davis, S. (2015). The "Strong Black Woman Collective": A Developing Theoretical Framework for Understanding Collective Communication Practices of Black Women. Women's Studies in Communication, 38:20–35.

5. Throughout this book we use the terms black and white to refer to African Americans and to European Americans respectively.

6. Ibid.

7. Ibid.

8. Sanders, T. (2005). The Likeability Factor: How to Boost Your L-Factor and Achieve Your Life's Dreams. NY: Crown Publishers.

9. Catalyst (2007). The Double-Bind Dilemma for Women in Leadership: Damned if You Do, Doomed if You Don't. pp. 20. Retrieved on 3/1/2016 from http://www.catalyst.org/knowledge/ double-bind-dilemma-women-leadership-damned-if-you-do- doomed-if-you-dont-0.

10. Ibid.

11. Babcock, L. and Laschever, S. (2009). Ask for It: How Women Can Use the Power of Negotiation to Get What They Really Want. NY:Bantam Books.

12. Den Hartog, D. Assertiveness. In Culture, Leadership, and Organizations: The GLOBE Study of 62 Societies.

13. Li, P. (2014). Hitting the Ceiling: An Examination of Barriers to Success for Asian American Women. Berkeley Journal of Gender, Law & Justice.

14. Ibid.

15. Den Hartog, D. Assertiveness. In Culture, Leadership, and Organizations: The GLOBE Study of 62 Societies.

16. Ibid.

17. Rottenberg (2014). Crazy is a Compliment. The Power of Zigging When Everyone Else Zags. Portfolio.

Chapter 1: Difficult Conversations 101

1. Holmes, J. (1989). Sex differences and apologies: One aspect of communicative competence. Applied Linguistics, 10(2), 194-213.

2. Tannen, D. (2001). Stand up for Yourself at Work, At Home, In Life. Good Housekeeping, April.

3. Ibid.

4. Ban Bossy. Encourage girls to lead. Retrieved on 2/25/2016 from BanBossy.com.

5. Kohlberg, L. (1984). Essays on moral development: Vol. 2. The psychology of moral development. NY: Harper.

6. Craske, M. and Chowdhury, N. Why Are Women Anxious and Worried More Often Than Men? In Hazlett-Stevens, H. (2005). Women Who Worry Too Much: How to Stop Worry and Anxiety from Ruining Relationships, Work & Fun. Harbinger Publications, Inc.

Chapter 2: Fears and Worries

1. Hazlett-Stevens, H. (2005). Women Who Worry Too Much: How to Stop Worry and Anxiety from Ruining Relationships, Work & Fun. NY:Harbinger Publications, Inc.

2. Hazlett-Stevens, H. (2005). Women Who Worry Too Much: How to Stop Worry and Anxiety from Ruining Relationships, Work & Fun. Harbinger Publications, Inc.

3. Pittman, C. & Karle, E. (2015). Rewire Your Anxious Brain: How to use the neuroscience of fear to end anxiety, panic & worry. New Harbinger Publications.

4. Hazlett-Stevens, H. (2005). Women Who Worry Too Much: How to Stop Worry and Anxiety from Ruining Relationships, Work & Fun. Harbinger Publications, Inc.

5. Ursini, T. (2003). The Cowards Guide to Conflict: Empowering Solutions for Those Who Would Rather Run Than Fight. Sourcebooks, Inc.

6. Evans, G. (2000). Play Like a Man, Win Like a Women: What Men Know About Success that Women Need to Learn. NY:Broadway Books.

7. Mackey, R., & O'Brien, B. (1998). Marital Conflict Management: Gender and Ethnic Differences. Social Work, 43(2), 128-141.

8. Markus, H.R., & Conner, A. (2013). Clash! 8 Cultural Conflicts that Make Us Who We Are. Hudson Street Press.

9. Anderson, T. (2015). Index funds trounce actively managed funds: Study. The Morningstar Investment Conference. Retrieved on 2/28/2017 from http://www.cnbc.com/2015/06/26/index-funds- trounce-actively-managed-funds-study.html.

10. Holliday, K. (2013). This industry has an entry level salary of $335,000. CNBC. Retrieved on 2/27/2016 from http://www.cnbc.com/2013/11/01/this-industry-has-an-entry-level-salary-of-335000.html.

11. Evans (2000). Play Like a Man, Win Like a Woman: What Men Know About Success Than Women Need to Learn. NY:Broadway Books.

12. Tarr-Whelan, L. (2009). Women Lead the Way: Your Guide to Stepping Up to Leadership and Changing the World. Berrett-Koehler Publishers, Inc.

13. McGregor, J. (2015). Among professional women, African Americans are most likely to want top executive jobs, report says. The Washington Post. Retrieved on 2/28/2016 from https://www.washingtonpost. com/news/on-leadership/wp/2015/04/22/among-professional- women-african-americans-are-most-likely-to-want-top-executive- jobs-report-says/.

14. Evans (2000). Play Like a Man, Win Like a Woman: What Men Know About Success Than Women Need to Learn. NY:Broadway Books.

15. Ibid.

16. Ibid.

17. Ibid.

18. Lieberman, D.J., Ph.D. (1998). Instant Analysis: How to Understand and Change the 100 Most Common, Annoying, Puzzling, Self-Defeating Behaviors and Habits. NY:ST. Amrtin's Griffin.

19. Selk, J. (2013). Habit Formation: The 21-Day Myth. Forbes Online. Retrieved on 6/18/2016 from http://www.forbes.com/sites/jasonselk/2013/04/15/habit-formation-the-21-day-myth/#2472005d6fed

Chapter 3: Do This *Before* the Difficult Conversation

1. Forward, S. (1986). Men Who Hate Women & the Women Who Love Them: When Loving Hurts and You Don't Know Why. NY:Bantam Books.

2. Seligman, M. (2007). What You Can Change and What You Can't: The Complete Guide to Successful Self-Improvement. NY:Vintage Books.

3. Benenson, J., Khun, M., Ryan, P., Ferranti, A., et. al. (2014). Human Males Appear More Prepared Than Females to Resolve Conflicts with Same-Sex Peers. Hum Nat (25), 251-268.

4. Schuman, K. & Ross, M. (2010). Why Women Apologize More Than Men: Gender Differences in Thresholds for Perceiving Offensive Behavior. Psychological Science 21(11) 1649–1655.

5. Beazley, C. (2010). The Many Sides of Optimism. Retrieved on 2/14/2016 from http://positivepsychology.org.uk/pp-theory/optimism/97-the-many-sides-of-optimism.html.

6. Chodron, P. (2001). Start Where You Are: A Guide to Compassionate Living (Shambhala Classics). NY:Shambala.

7. Pollan, S. & Levine, M. (2004). *Lifescripts: What to Say to Get What You Want in Life's Toughest Situations*. NY:Wiley.

8. Cuddy , A. (2012). Your Body Language Shapes Who You Are. TED talk retrieved on 3/7/2016 from http://www.ted.com/talks/amy_cuddy_your_body_language_shapes_who_you_are.

Chapter 4: The NO FEAR™ Method

1. Seligman, M. (2007). What You Can Change and What You Can't: The Complete Guide to Successful Self-Improvement. NY:Vintage Books.

2. Sanders, T. (2005). The Likeability Factor: How to Boost Your L-Factor and Achieve Your Life's Dreams. NY:Crown Publishers.

Chapter 6: What to Do During the Difficult Conversation

1. Kofman, F. Managing Difficult Conversations. Retrieved on 2/26/2016 from http://leanin.org/education/managing-difficult-conversations/.

2. Babcock, L. and Laschever, S. (2009). Ask for It: How Women Can Use the Power of Negotiation to Get What They Really Want. NY:Bantam Books.

3. Sandberg, S. (2013). Lean In: Women, Work, and the Will to Lead. NY: Knopf.

4. Babcock, L. and Laschever, S. (2009). Ask for It: How Women Can Use the Power of Negotiation to Get What They Really Want. NY:Bantam Books.

5. Butler, D., & Geis, F. L. (1990). Nonverbal affect responses to male and female leaders: Implications for leadership evaluations. Journal of Personality and Social Psychology, 58, 48–59.

6. Davis, M., Capobianco, S. & Kraus, L. (2010). Gender Differences in Responding to Conflict in the Workplace: Evidence from a Large Sample of Working Adults. Sex Roles 63:500–514. Springer.

7. Myers, D. (2014). Psychology, Second Edition. NY:Worth Publishers.

8. Ibid.

9. Fox Cabane, O. (2013). The Charisma Myth: How Anyone Can Master the Art and Science of Personal Magnetism. NY: The Penguin Group.

10. Turaga, R. (2015). Managing Difficult Workplace Conversations. Online Learning Solutions. Telangana, India.

Chapter 7: Keep Your Emotions Under Control

1. Ronson, J. (2012). The Psychopath Test: A Journey Through the Madness Industry. NY:Riverhead Books.

2. Bercovici, J, (2011). Why (Some) Psychopaths Make Great CEOs. Forbes Business. Retrieved on 2/27/2016 from http://www.forbes.com/sites/jeffbercovici/2011/06/14/why-some-psychopaths- make-great-ceos/#497388174fac.

3. AboutNews (2016). Characteristics of the Psychopathic Personality. Retrieved on 2/17/2016 from http://crime.about.com/od/serial/a/psychopaths.htm.

4. The End of Rational Vs. Emotional: How Both Logic and Feeling Play Key Roles in Marketing and Decision Making. Retrieved on 2/272/1016 from http://www.fastcocreate.com/1682962/the-end-of-rational-vs-emotional-how-both-logic-and-feeling-play-key-roles-in-marketing-and-.

5. Van Praet, D. (2014). Unconscious Branding: How Neuroscience Can Empower (and Inspire) Marketing. NY:St. Martin's Griffin.

6. If you want to know more let me recommend four of my all times favorite books: Subliminal: How your Unconscious Mind Rules Your Behavior, by

Leonard Mlodinow; Predictably Irrational: The hidden forces that shape our decisions, by Dan Ariely; Decisive: How to Make Better Choices in Life and in Work, by the Heath brothers Chip and Dan; and Blind Spots, by Mike H. Bazerman.

7. Hervey, C. (1995). The mask of sanity: An attempt to clarify some issues about the so-called psychopathic personality. St Louis, MO, US: C V Mosby Co.

8. Van Praet, D. (2014). Unconscious Branding: How Neuroscience Can Empower (and Inspire) Marketing. NY:St. Martin's Griffin

9. As summarized in the article Are Women Too Emotional? Published by The Center for Women in Business (CWB), a program of the U.S. Chamber of Commerce Foundation. Retrieved on 2/27/2016 from https://www.uschamberfoundation.org/blog/post/are-women-too-emotional/32277

10. Ibid.

11. Myers, D. (2014). Psychology for AP. NY:Worth Publishers.

12. Ibid.

13. As summarized in the article Are Women Too Emsotional? Published by The Center for Women in Busines (CWB), a program of the U.S. Chamber of Commerce Foundation. Retrieved on 2/27/2016 from https://www.uschamberfoundation.org/blog/post/are-women-too-emotional/32277

14. Lalama, C. (2004). Are Women More Emotional than Men? Women's Studies Center, Florida International University. Volume 2.

15. Ibid.

16. Ibid.

17. Feldman Barrett, L., Lane, R., Sechrest, L., & Schwartz, G. (2000). Sex differences in emotional awareness. Personality and Social Psychology Bulletin. 26(9), 1027-1035.

18. Feldman-Barret, L., & Bliss Moreau, E. (2009). She's Emotional. He's Having a Bad Day: Attributional Explanations for Emotion Stereotypes. Emotion, Vol. 9, No. 5, 649–658.

19. McGlowan-Fellows, B., & Thomas, C. S. (2005). Changing roles: Corporate mentoring of Black women. International Journal of Mental Health, 33, 3–18.

20. Ibid.

21. Cionea, I., Tanan Johnson, A., Bruscella, J., & Van Gilder, B. (2015). Taking Conflict Personally and the Use of the Demand/Withdraw Pattern of Intraethnic Serial Arguments. Argumentation and Advocacy 52: 32-43.

22. Hample, D., & Dallinger, J. M. (1995). A Lewinian perspective on taking conflict personally: Revision, refinement, and validation of the instrument. Communication Quarterly, 43, 297-319.

23. Adapted from a revised TCP Scale instrument developed by Hample, D. and Dallinger, J. M. (1995).

24. Hample, D., & Dallinger, J. M. (1993). The Effects of Taking Conflicts Personally on Arguing Behavior. Conference Proceedings, National Communication Association/American Forensic Association.

25. Ibid.

26. Ibid.

Chapter 8: What Not to Do *During* the Difficult Conversation

1. Dieken, C. (2009). Talk Less, Say More: 3 Habits to Influence Others and Make Things Happen. John Wiley & Sons, Inc.

2. Working with Different Communication Styles. The College of St. Scholastica, Duluth, MN. Retrieved on 2/25/2016 from http:// resources.css.edu/diversityservices /docs/comminicationstyles.pdf

3. Continua of Communication Styles. Intercultural Communication I. World YMCA. Retrieved on 2/25/2016 from http://www.ymca. int/fileadmin/library/6_Communications/1_General_Tools/ Intercultural_Communication_1.pdf.

4. Differences Between Linear and Circular Communication Styles. Interpersonal and Corporate Communication Center. Retrieved on 2/15/2016 from http://work911.com/communication/styles-lin-circt.htm.

5. Tannen, D. (1999). Contrite makes right. Civilization, 6, May/June.

6. Schuman, K. & Ross, M. (2010). Why Women Apologize More Than Men: Gender Differences in Thresholds for Perceiving Offensive Behavior. Psychological Science 21(11) 1649–1655.

7. Engel, B. (2001). The power of apology. NY: Wiley.

8. Ibid.

9. Ibid.

10. Robb, A. (2015). Why Men Are Prone to Interrupting Women. Retrieved on 2/14/2015 from http://nytlive.nytimes.com/womenintheworld/2015/03/19/google-chief-blasted-for-repeatedly-in-terrupting-female-government-official/.

11. Kofman, F. Managing Difficult Conversations. Retrieved on 2/26/2016 from http://leanin.org/education/managing-difficult-conversations/.

12. http://www.stickk.com/faq/about/About+stickK.

Chapter 9: What to Do *After* the Difficult Conversation

1. Miller, A., Worthington, E., & McDaniel, M. (2008). *Gender and Forgiveness: A meta-analytic review and research agenda.* Journal of Social and Clinical Psychology, 27(8), 843–876.

2. Laseter, I. (2010). Words That Works in Business: A Practical Guide to Effective Communication in the Workplace. NY:Puddle Dancer Press.

3. Davis, M., Capobianco, S. & Kraus, L. (2010). Gender Differences in Responding to Conflict in the Workplace: Evidence from a Large Sample of Working Adults. Sex Roles (2010) 63:500–514

4. Hazlett-Stevens, H. (2005). Women Who Worry Too Much: How to Stop Worry and Anxiety from Ruining Relationships, Work & Fun. NY:Harbinger Publications, Inc.

One Last Word

1. Sarsons, H. (2015). *Gender Differences in Recognition for Group Work*. Retrieved on 6/19/2016 from http://scholar.harvard.edu/files/sarsons/files/gender_groupwork.pdf?m=1449178759

CPSIA information can be obtained at www.ICGtesting.com
Printed in the USA
LVOW10s2330041016

507440LV00011B/105/P